White Foreigners.

THE

WHITE FOREIGNERS

FROM OVER THE WATER.

THE STORY OF THE AMERICAN MISSION TO THE BURMESE AND THE KARENS.

PUBLISHED BY THE
AMERICAN TRACT SOCIETY,
150 NASSAU-STEET, NEW YORK.

PREFACE.

THE stories in this little book are true. It gives an account of the manner in which a down-trodden people received the gospel. They told the missionaries they had been waiting for "White Foreigners from over the water" to bring them God's Book; their fathers had bidden them expect happiness to reach them in this way.

You like to read of great conquerors and brave soldiers. Here is the story of some of the conquests of Jesus, the Prince of Peace, and of some of the faithful soldiers who have fought under his banner. Nobler battles these than any to which mortal kings have led their followers; far braver soldiers these, who have willingly and cheerfully suffered years of privation and persecution for the love they bore to their Saviour and Lord. The kings of the earth kill to conquer; the King of Heaven died to save.

The Son of God goes forth to war,
  A kingly crown to gain;
His blood-red banner streams afar,
  Who follows in his train?

A noble army, men and boys,
  The matron and the maid,
Around the Saviour's throne rejoice,
  In robes of light arrayed.

They climbed the steep ascent of heaven
  Through peril, toil, and pain;
O God, to us may grace be given,
  To follow in their train.

CONTENTS.

THE WHITE FOREIGNERS.

CHAPTER I.

BURMAH, WITH ITS ANIMALS AND PLANTS.

BURMAH is a country a little farther distant than India is. In the north it touches India, and is sometimes spoken of as Farther India. No doubt you can point to it on the map of the world, and know that the broad waters of the Bay of Bengal wash its shores.

Burmah is a warm, pleasant, and beautiful land, with high mountains, wide plains, deep fertile valleys, and broad rivers. A great number of people dwell in it, either in cities built along the river banks, or in smaller towns and villages scattered over the country.

The largest river in Burmah is the Irrawadi, which runs through the country, and divides into a number of channels or mouths where it enters the Bay of Bengal. A good many cities and towns are built upon its banks: Ava, Prome, Rangoon, Bassein, and many more. Another river, the Salween, flows very much in the same direction, and at its mouth are built Amherst and Maulmain. Between the Irrawadi and the Salween is another river, the Sittang, upon the banks of which the old city of Tounghoo is situated. Lower down on the seacoast are Tavoy and Mergui, and to the north lies the province of Arracan.

But the towns and villages, and the cultivated land around them, by no means fill the country. There are vast jungles and forests, in which wild beasts roam at pleasure. Tigers, leopards, elephants, buffaloes, wild hogs and oxen, and many kinds of deer are found in the land. They are not all creatures that you would wish to meet, are they? unless, indeed, you were well armed and prepared for them, then a hunt might be pleasant.

The elephants are sometimes hunted for the sake of their tusks; and many are caught and tamed and forced to work for their owners. I am sure you have often heard stories of elephants, and know what sensible creatures they are. White elephants are very much prized, and the kings always like to possess one or more, and to have the title of "Lord of the white elephant."

Men are sometimes eaten by the tigers. These animals do not, like the wild elephants, keep far away from the villages, but will venture quite close to them, and will even enter the compounds, that is, the house enclosures. If once a tiger has eaten human flesh, and finds out how nice it is, he will always try to get more, and then it is very dangerous to meet him.

Once a missionary reached a lonely cabin just at dusk, and was surprised to find it closely barricaded all around. He called to the men who were inside, and asked of what enemy they were afraid, that they should shut themselves in so closely. They told him that the day before a man had been eaten by a tiger close by. When this was known, five men had armed themselves, and had gone out to hunt and kill the animal. They found the track, and were following it; but instead of succeeding in killing the tiger, he had come out boldly on to the plain, and had actually leaped upon one of his pursuers, and devoured him also. The other four had returned to their hut, and, for fear the tiger should attack them, had barricaded themselves in. As it was already dusk, I should think the missionary must have been glad to take refuge with them for the night. A tiger once actually walked into a wayside shed and carried off a young man who was sleeping among a number of others.

Leopards also attack men, and will even climb trees. Two men were overtaken by night in the forests near Maulmain. No house was near, so they climbed a large tree and went to sleep among the branches. One man was on a low branch, and by-and-by he was awakened by something creeping along the branch above him. From what he could distinguish of the dusky form in the darkness, he thought it was a tiger. He was not far wrong; it was a leopard. He called to his sleeping companion, the man answered, and the leopard was perfectly still for a few minutes—not a claw moved. But though the man had answered, he was not aroused, and was sound asleep again directly. His companion dared not go to him, and in a little time the leopard seized him, and jumping down with him, ate him there at the foot of the tree.

The rhinoceros is as much feared as the tiger, and this animal is very common. If it is once provoked, it will not leave its enemy; and it is so thickly covered with hard skin that it is not easy to kill. If a man, to escape the rage of a rhinoceros, climbs a tree, it is said that the huge creature will remain at its foot for three or four days without once quitting its post. Rhinoceroses like muddy places in which they can roll about, and they are met with mostly on the river banks, though they sometimes roam over the mountains. The Chinese buy rhinoceros horns for medicine: I cannot tell you for what diseases they use them.

There are plenty of monkeys of different kinds among the trees, gibbering and chattering. One species, the long-armed ape, is very plentiful, and these monkeys have a habit of screaming as soon as the day dawns. There is a monkey, too, which abounds on the sea-shore, called the fisher-monkey. It feeds upon crabs and shell-fish. The fisher-monkeys come down in troops when the tide is low, to hunt; and there you might see them, some busy turning over the stones, others breaking open shells, or thrusting their arms into the sand to dig out the crabs which have buried themselves to escape their foes. These monkeys like fruit as well as fish. Once a missionary, Dr. Mason, was passing near the shore in a boat, and a troop of fisher-monkeys followed him for some distance to get the plantains which he threw into the water for them.

There are also large numbers of squirrels and bats. The largest kind of bat is called the flying-fox, and sometimes it measures more than a yard across the wings from tip to tip. These bats are very fond of fruit, and steal it wherever they can. In some parts of the country they may be seen, many of them together, hanging by their heels, as is the custom of bats, from the tops of the palm-trees. The bats which get into houses are smaller. You will by-and-by read of a house in which there were a great number of these troublesome creatures.

Of birds there are many, such as vultures, eagles, kites, buzzards, falcons, owls, hawks, and crows. Crows are so plentiful everywhere, that women, when carrying fruit, always have a stick to drive them away. They are very bold indeed. One pleasant morning a gentleman was sitting in his verandah, sipping coffee. His toast was on the table by his side, and he was enjoying the cool freshness of the morning air. For a minute he turned away to speak to some one, and on looking round again he discovered that a greedy crow had actually carried his toast away. Don't you think it must have been crows that Pharaoh's baker, of whom we read in the Bible, saw in his dream devouring the baked meats out of the basket on his head?

Then there are birds of a different kind, such as wagtails, finches, larks, hornbills, tailor-birds, cuckoos; and one, the paradise edolius, is a very beautiful singer. There are parrots, peacocks, pheasants, partridges, pigeons, quails, turtle-doves, and wild fowl. By the rivers and seaside you would find adjutants, bitterns, ibises, herons, rails, snipes, oyster-catchers, teals, pelicans, cormorants, scissors-bills, and many more. Some of these you know as English birds; but though they have the same name, and are of similar kinds, most of them are of different species from those we see here. The parrots often come down in great flocks upon the rice-fields, and are very destructive. Pelicans, too, are seen in flocks of from fifty to a hundred. The birds' nests which are eaten by the Chinese are found on the coast near Tavoy; they are built by a species of swallow in limestone caves, and are collected by the natives for sale.

Crocodiles, turtles, lizards, serpents, and frogs abound. Some of the lizards are useful for killing rats; but they are at the same time very disagreeable, because they get so much into the houses: you could never be sure, if you were eating your dinner in Burmah, that a lizard would not drop down from the ceiling on to the table. Some of the lizards are eaten for food.

Insects are very plentiful. Here are the names of some: tiger-beetles, long-snouted beetles, capricorn-beetles, camelopard, lady-bird, musk, and chameleon beetles. The wing-cases of the chameleon-beetle are very beautiful, and are used for necklaces, or mixed with flowers for head-ornaments. The capricorn-beetle is more than two inches long, and sometimes flies into the houses at Maulmain. Here are glowworms, fireflies, blister-flies, locusts, soothsayers, the walking-stick and walking-leaf insects, ants, butterflies, spiders, and ant-lions, which make pits for other insects. One species of the walking-stick insect is nearly twelve inches long. The soothsayers, or mantis, are considered very pious insects, because they hold their fore-feet together as though they were praying. Xavier, it is said, once seeing a mantis moving along in its solemn way, told it to sing hymns, and immediately it began to sing. I don't think any one has heard it since. The white ants are very troublesome in the houses, destroying every thing. At one time of the year they come into the houses in such numbers that people are glad to go anywhere to be out of their way.

Large books have been written describing these living creatures and their wonderful habits, and still there is a great deal to tell. "The works of the Lord are great, sought out of all those who have pleasure therein." These beasts and birds and insects are some of his works; and I hope you find pleasure in seeking out as much knowledge concerning them as possible.

I must just say a word about the plants of Burmah. There are many fine timber-trees growing in the forests; one of the principal is the teak-tree, the wood of which is very hard, and another is the ironwood-tree. Then there are pine and palms of many kinds; and trees bearing most gorgeous flowers and most luscious fruits, such as jacks, breadfruit-trees, tamarinds, mulberries, citrons, oranges, guavas, mangoes, cocoa-nuts, cashew-nuts, and many more. There are vegetables and flowers in plenty for the gardens and fields: yams, beans, potatoes, tomatoes, mushrooms, pineapples, wheat, maize, rice, and so on. Ferns, mosses, and orchids grow in great luxuriance, and in wet seasons so quickly do they grow that long fern-fronds are sometimes seen hanging from the half-finished brick-work of the pagodas, where masons were at work not many weeks before. The orchids are peculiarly beautiful on account of their lovely fragrant flowers; many of these which grow as wild-flowers in Burmah are cultivated in England with great care in hothouses.

These are a few, and but very few, of the plants found in Burmah; but it will be enough to show how fertile a land it must be, a land in which God has made most ample provision for the wants of man.

CHAPTER II.

THE RELIGION AND CUSTOMS OF THE BURMESE.

WHEN God placed man on the earth, he blessed him, and said: "Have dominion over the fish of the sea, and over the fowl of the air, and over every living thing that moveth upon the earth. Behold, I have given you every herb bearing seed which is upon the face of all the earth, and every tree, in the which is the fruit of a tree yielding seed, to you it shall be for meat." "And God breathed into his nostrils the breath of life, and man became a living soul."

For many hundreds of years the inhabitants of Burmah have lived in their beautiful land, surrounded on every side with blessings which God has given to them, but God they have forgotten. "Their idols are silver and gold, the work of men's hands; they have mouths, but they speak not; eyes have they, but they see not; they have ears, but they hear not; noses have they, but they smell not; they have hands, but they handle not; feet have they, but they walk not; neither speak they through their throats."

The religion of Burmah is Buddhism. This is the religion not only of Burmah, but of many of the inhabitants of China, Siam, Tartary, and Ceylon. It is computed that there are as many as four hundred millions of people in the world who are worshippers of Buddha.

I could not explain to you all that the Buddhists believe. A Buddh is one who has made himself a god by his own virtues and by practising great self-denial. They say that already, since the beginning of time, there have been four great Buddhs—Kanthathan, Gaunagon, Kathapa, and Gaudama.

The last, Gaudama, is the one they worship now. They believe he was in existence for many ages before he became a man, but not as a god. Once he was a tiger, at one time a deer, at another an elephant; at one time he ruled in heaven, and at another in hell.

At last he was born as a child in India; and when we compare the Burmese dates with our own, we find that this is said to have happened about six hundred years before Christ came to the earth, and about the time that the ten tribes were carried captive from Palestine to be scattered and sown among the nations of the earth.

Gaudama, the Burmese say, was born under a tree now called the Amherstia, and that as soon as he was born he got up, walked seven steps, and with a voice like the roaring of the king of lions exclaimed: "I am the most excellent of men. I am the most famous of men. I am the most victorious of men." If this account were true, he must certainly have been very different from ordinary babies.

He was the son of a great Indian monarch; but, instead of living in ease and luxury at his father's court, he fled away into the wilderness, where he practised very great self-denial. Many stories are told of the wonderful things that happened to him, but at last, when he was eighty years old, he died.

And now do you suppose the Buddhists

think Gaudama is in heaven? Not at all; they believe he has gone out of existence altogether. They could not tell you any thing about where their god is, and yet they worship him, and say they are to worship him for five thousand years. When the five thousand years are ended, they expect another Buddh, named Aremaday, and he is to flourish eighty thousand years.

Some of the doctrines that Gaudama taught are very good. His great commands to his followers are these: "Kill not; steal not; commit no uncleanness; lie not; drink no intoxicating liquor."

The Buddhists, you will say, if they keep these commands, are not bad people. Some of his commands are the very same that God gave to the Jews on Mount Sinai.

But they do not keep them. They make images of Gaudama and place them in temples; they bring offerings of gold-leaf and flowers, of umbrellas and crackers, to show their devotion to him. They build pagodas over his relics, and expend large sums of money in gilding them handsomely. They support priests, who preach to them about him in the zayats; all this they do, and yet do not obey his commands.

Are you surprised? Do we obey the commands of our God? No, they are broken; you break them every day; and yet a great many of us try very hard to do as God would have us do.

But, you will say, our religion is quite different from theirs; ours is the true God, and theirs is a false god. That is true; and there is one great difference between the true religion and all false religions: this difference lies in the two words, love and fear.

The great commands of God's religion are these: "Thou shalt love the Lord thy God with all thy heart, and with all thy soul, and with all thy strength, and with all thy mind, and thy neighbor as thyself." "This do, and thou shalt live."

And then when we sinned, and did not obey these commands, and were worthy of nothing but death: "God so loved the world, that he gave his only-begotten Son, that whosoever believeth in him should not perish, but have everlasting life." Now the two great commandments are: "Believe on the name of his

Son Jesus Christ," and, "Love one another." And Jesus says to us—Jesus who has died for us: "If ye love me, keep my commandments." Should we not answer: "We have known and believed the love that God hath to us;" "we love him because he first loved us?" His commandments, which are all embraced in that one word, "love," are not grievous.

This, in short, is the religion the Bible teaches. The Buddhists know no Redeemer who has died to save them, though they are aware they constantly sin; they know nothing of God's love and a Saviour's compassion, and life everlasting with him. Their religion is a religion of fear. They fear that when they die they shall again come into the world as a lion or a toad, a lizard or a rhinoceros, and believe that the better they are the sooner they shall come to what they call nigban, or a state in which they shall not exist at all.

The priests of the Buddhists in Burmah are more like monks than priests. They are called pongyees, and dwell in houses or kyoungs, apart from the people. These pongyees may not marry, and ought not even to look at a woman. The rules they have to observe about women are so strict, that if a pongyee were to pass by a place where his own mother had fallen into the river, he might not put out his hands to assist her in her efforts to reach the bank. If no one else were near, he might, rather than allow her to drown, reach a pole or a stick to her to take hold of; but then he must think it is nothing more than a log he is dragging out of the water. It must, you see, be difficult to be a good son and a good pongyee at the same time.

One day a priest from Ava called upon a missionary's wife—Mrs. Mason. She entered the room in which he was, and immediately the pongyee took a seat upon the table. Mrs. Mason did not approve of such manners, but she knew it was only in order to keep his head above hers that her visitor had chosen such a seat; therefore she called for a mat and pillow for herself, and sat down upon the floor. Seeing her so low, he consented to move and sit down also. This priest had called to talk with Mrs. Mason about the Christian religion. She handed him a copy of the Bible in Burmese. He asked her to lay it on the mat for him to take, as he dared not defile himself by receiving it from her her hand. This she did, and then he took the book and read portions of it aloud.

The pongyees dress in yellow robes and go about with shaven heads and bare feet. Some carry rice-pots round the towns in the mornings, and go from door to door begging for food; or, rather, they do not beg, but stand outside and wait till food is brought. They only eat once a day, and are not allowed to have gold or silver or ornaments.

In the kyoungs the boys are taught to read; and the pongyees are their teachers. The books they use do not resemble ours, but are written on palm-leaves. They have no slates or pencils or maps. They are principally taught to read the stories of Gaudama's life, and what is written in the sacred books about him and those who have refused to believe in him. When they go to school they wear a yellow dress like their teachers; but this is not all the year round. The Burmese boys go to school in the rainy season, as the Scotch boys do in winter; but in the dry, warm weather they are either helping their fathers or amusing themselves.

Sometimes the priests preach to the people in the zayats, and here too they do very little

more than recount the stories about Gaudama. The zayats are open sheds. They are built in all the towns and along the highroads of the country. They are used as inns and market-places, and any one may go in and rest, or lie down and sleep in them. At Tavoy there is a very fine zayat.

There are in Burmah many immense images of Gaudama, and the temples are crowded with them. At the new and full moon the people go up to worship; and from July to October they are very strict in their religious observances; indeed, they make that time a kind of Lent. In October, especially, they hold many religious festivals, and flock to the places where there are the most famous pagodas and temples. The pagodas hold the relics of Gaudama, the temples his images.

Numbers of boats filled with gayly-dressed people may be seen at these festival-times gliding over the waters of the rivers; and while listening to the music from the bands on board, you would suppose any thing rather than that these people were going to worship. But when they reach the temples they at once become grave, and hasten in with their offerings and say their prayers as quickly as possible. I am afraid, although these people do it gravely, you and I would be inclined to laugh at the scenes in the temples. Some men may be seen gluing gold-leaf upon the faces of the images, and others letting off crackers in their honor.

The number of paper umbrellas, fruits, and flowers, brought as offerings, is enormous. At one temple—but this was in Ceylon, not in Burmah—it is said that 6,480,320 flowers were brought on one occasion. I should like to know who counted them. The umbrellas are sometimes white, sometimes gold and white, sometimes they are made of many different colored papers. But of what use these crackers, which fill the temples with smoke and noise, and these fruits and flowers and umbrellas scattered about in all directions—of what use they can be, you and I would find it difficult to imagine.

How different these offerings from those our God asks of us! "My son," he says, "give me thy heart." "A broken and a contrite heart, O God, thou wilt not despise." All other offerings Christ our Saviour made for us when he offered himself without spot to God.

We have spoken of kyoungs, zayats, temples, and pagodas, but have said nothing about the houses. Many of the houses are nothing but little bamboo dwellings, raised by posts a few feet from the ground. There is no cold to keep out, and the builders are not careful to make the walls air-tight. The bamboos are put up rough, and there are generally plenty of crevices through which the inhabitants can look out without troubling about windows. The floors of these houses are made of woven bamboo, and are elastic, which would be to us uncomfortable for walking on. The roofs are thatched with the leaves of the water-palm, and most of the houses have a verandah. In the large towns there are some board and some brick houses, but most of the native dwellings are these slight bamboo buildings.

The men wear a long cloth, called a putso, wound around their bodies; the women wear a smaller piece, called a terminé; and both use a white linen jacket, called an ingie. Men, women, and children all smoke.

Have you noticed that I have told you only of boys in the schools and of men in the temples? Do you want to know where the girls are taught and where the women worship? Women and girls are not taught to read at all, and they worship outside the temples; they are not considered worthy to come inside. The women are the slaves, not the companions of the men. They work hard, and do many things which in this country we think fit only for laboring men to do. No Burmese woman is permitted to leave the country.

Besides the Burmese there are other tribes dwelling in Burmah; one especially, the Karen nation, is scattered far and wide over the land. The Karens have been conquered by the Burmese, and are heavily taxed and cruelly oppressed by them.

The Karens do not worship Gaudama; they believe there are a great many gods, a god of the earth, a god of the land, a god of the waters, a god of the sun, a god of the moon, a god of the trees, a god of the woods, and so on. They are great believers in ghosts, too, and fear them very much; but they have another belief that is really wonderful, a belief that from over the sea white foreigners are to come with a book to teach them about the true God.

If you did not know it before, you will have

learned since you began to read this little book, that the white foreigners have gone to Burmah with God's book; for I have mentioned the missionaries and the Burmese Bible; and I hope you will be interested in the account I have written for you of the first Protestant missionaries in this far-away land, their trials and difficulties, their sorrows and successes.

I say Protestant missionaries, for Roman-catholics had been in Burmah before them. They, however, had not done much in the way of teaching the natives. The first converts were cruelly persecuted by their friends; and when they found this they left off trying to convert the subjects of the Burmese kings.

It seemed quite possible too that the inhabitants of Burmah had heard of the true God—the Karens certainly had—long, long before either Roman-catholic or Protestant could have visited them.

Did you ever consider where that land of Tarshish was to which King Solomon's navy sailed once in three years? It must have been a land in which there were peacocks, apes, elephants, gold, and silver. All these things are found plentifully in Burmah. Many people believe that Burmah is the land called Tarshish in the Bible; and I think it is very likely.

If so, and King Solomon's ships really sailed up those rivers, the Irrawadi and the Salween, you may be quite sure that the Hebrew sailors and the Burmese people found some way of talking to each other, and we can pretty well guess what they would talk about.

The Burmese would ask for what purpose the strangers wanted the gold and silver, the peacocks, ivory, and apes.

Then the Hebrews, proud of their great king and his riches, would tell how Solomon was building a splendid temple for the worship of their God, and was enriching it with gold. That he was making a great many vessels of gold and silver, and a wonderful ivory throne for himself, which was to be covered with the best gold, and to have a golden footstool, and to have twelve lions standing on the steps. It was for making these things they wanted the gold and ivory. The apes and peacocks would ornament his gardens, and be given as presents to his friends.

When the Burmese heard all this, they would ask more. They would want to know what God it was this great king worshipped. They would hear it was the God who made heaven and earth. And then would follow the story of the garden of Eden, and of Adam and Eve; of Abraham, Isaac, Jacob, and Joseph; of the flight of the Israelites from Egypt; of the ten commandments given in the fire and cloud on Mount Sinai; of the land in which they now lived; and of the promise God had given of a Saviour yet to come, for whom they were waiting and watching.

Does it not appear possible that in those times, long, long ago, the Burmese heard all this from the Hebrew sailors who very likely came to their shores? And if it was not in this way, how was it that the Karens came to believe in white foreigners with God's book, and to know, as they certainly did, the story of Adam and Eve?

It may have been in other ways, for the Karens say they once had books. But we will leave these difficult questions for those who know more than we do, and pass on to something more easy.

CHAPTER III.

Two Burmese Legends.

THE Burmese are very fond of tales and legends. Many of these are amusing, and others are instructive. The priests tell many such tales, which have come down from one generation to another. Perhaps you would like to hear some of these old-world stories. I do not wish you to believe them.

STORY OF KING TEKTHA.

Once upon a time there lived in Burmah a king named Tektha.

The kings that went before him had been devout worshippers of Gaudama, and had listened to what their teachers and priests taught them. But Tektha did not believe in Gaudama, but listened to strange teachers, who taught him that every thing was God.

He would not hear the Buddhist books, nor worship the relics nor the images. More than this, instead of behaving reverently to the priests, he destroyed their temples, and threw the idols into the water. He forbade his subjects also to worship Gaudama, and threatened that if they did they should be severely punished.

The people were in dismay. It was of no use for the priests to carry round their rice-pots; no one dared offer them food; the temples and pagodas were falling into ruins, and the images of Gaudama were lying in the water, spoilt and decaying.

What would be the consequence of this terrible treatment of their god? The people were afraid of the punishment with which the king threatened them if they worshipped Gaudama; they feared the evils the great spirits—the *nats*—might bring upon them if they did not.

But a few of the people would not give up the worship to which they had been so long accustomed, and among those who still in secret held to the old faith was a girl, twelve years of age, and her mother. I do not know the girl's name; but, said she, "The king has thrown the idols into the water because he is afraid of them." This was considered a very bold speech.

Affairs continued in this state for four years. When the girl was sixteen, she happened one day to be bathing in a tank with a number of her companions, and while amusing herself in the water, she saw an idol lying near. She ordered her attendants to lift it out and carry it to a zayat that was at hand. They reminded her that she would certainly be put to death for meddling with it; but she was very determined, and declared that she would worship that image as long as she lived. It was accordingly lifted out of the water, washed, and carried into the zayat.

A report of what had been done was immediately taken to the king, and you can imagine how enraged he was. He ordered his servants to take a fierce elephant, and make the animal trample this bold young woman to death.

But it was not so easy to do this. The seven principal *nats*, who had been greatly displeased by the king's wickedness, came to the defence of the girl. These seven were, the *nat* of the universe, the *nat* of the earth, the *nat* of the trees, the *nat* of the air, the *nat* of the cities, the *nat* of the villages, and the *nat* of the white umbrella.

The elephant was brought, but he did not touch the girl; he was beaten and goaded, but it was of no avail; he would not lift up a foot against her, and instead of being angry, only grew frightened, and tried to run away from her.

When the king heard that she could not be put to death this way, he ordered a quantity of straw—dry straw—to be collected, and the girl to be placed in the midst of it and burnt to death. The straw was brought, she was put in the middle, but no number of torches, no quantity of fire would make it burn. The *nats* were there, and they would not allow her to be put to death.

Then the king sent for her to his palace. He was surprised as well as angry now, and was wondering whether he might not possibly have been wrong in forsaking the gods of his forefathers. "If the image which you have dared to take from the water," said he, "will come through the air into my presence, and I see it, your life shall be spared; but if not, you shall be cut into seven pieces."

The young woman asked permission to return for a short time to the zayat. Her request was granted, and there she went and prayed very earnestly that the image might be carried into the king's presence. And lo, not only one, but eight images, and the young woman with her attendants, were immediately taken up by the *nats*, conveyed through the air, and put down before the king and his principal queen, his commander-in-chief, his officers, and a multitude of people. How they all shouted and wondered!

"Now," said the girl, turning to the king, "now that the image of my god and teacher has flown to you, will you order the teachers from whom you have learned this false religion to mount up also and fly through the air?"

The king ordered them to do so, but of course it was in vain; they could not fly. He was now convinced that the religion of Gaudama was the true religion; he compelled the false teachers to leave the country; the temples and images and pagodas were restored; this wonderful young woman he married, and made one of his principal queens; and King Tektha was for the remainder of his life a devoted Buddhist.

Stories that begin with "once upon a time" are not always true; and though the Burmese are taught such stories as these by their priests, you and I cannot believe them.

STORY OF THE WASHERMAN AND POTTER.*

In the olden time a potter conceived an evil design against a washerman, who lived with considerable ostentation; and being unable to bear the sight of wealth which the latter had acquired by washing clothes, he determined to come to an open rupture with him.

With this view he went to the king, and said: "Your majesty's royal elephant is black, but if you were to order the washerman to wash it white would you not become 'Lord of the white elephant?'" This speech was not made from any zeal for the king's

* From Winter's "Six Months in Burmah."

advantage, but because he thought that if the order were given to the washerman, according to his suggestion, and the elephant should not turn white after all, the fortune of the washerman would come to an end.

The king, on hearing the representation of the potter, took for granted it was sincere, and being deficient in wisdom, he, without consideration, sent for the washerman, and ordered him to wash the elephant white.

The washerman, seeing through the potter's design, replied: "Our art requires that, in order to bleach cloth, we should first put it in a boiler with soap and water, and then rub it well. In this manner only can your majesty's elephant be made white."

The king, considering that it was the potter's business, and not a washerman's, to make pots, called for the potter, and said to him: "Hey, you potter, a pot is required to lather my elephant in; go and make one large enough for the purpose."

The potter, on receiving this order, collected together all his friends and relations, and after they had accumulated a vast quantity of clay, he made a pot big enough to hold the elephant. When it was completed he showed it to the king, and it was delivered over to the washerman. The washerman put in soap and water, but as soon as the elephant placed his foot upon it, it broke to pieces.

After this, the potter made many others, but they were either too thick, so that the water could not be made to boil in them, or too thin, so that the first pressure of the elephant's foot mashed them to pieces. In this manner, being constantly employed, he was unable to attend to his business, and so he was utterly ruined.

MORAL.

Such as aim at the destruction of others, will find that their weapons will fail to reach those whom they intended, and will only recoil upon their own heads. Although a person be ever so poor, he ought not to design evil against others.

CHAPTER IV.

DR. JUDSON VISITS FRANCE, ENGLAND, AND INDIA, AND SETTLES AT RANGOON.

IT was at the time that Napoleon was emperor of France, and such sad and unchristian wars were carried on by him and other kings on the continent of Europe, that the first Protestant missionaries went to Burmah with the hope of teaching the Burmese the way of peace.

At Serampore, in India, there had been missionaries for several years; and in the year 1807 some of the good men who had been preaching and teaching there went to Rangoon, to establish a mission in that city.

While these first English missionaries were building themselves a house, and were hard at work learning the Burmese language, there was living in America a young man, in whose heart God had put the desire to become a missionary to the heathen. His parents were very sorry to find this was his wish, and they did all they could to prevent him from leaving them and his country. They told him how well he might get on if he stayed in his own land, how comfortable and happy and prosperous and rich he might be; while, if he became a missionary, he would be poor, and lead a life full of hardship and difficulty. But the more this young man prayed for help to do what was right, the more he felt he must become a missionary, and go wherever God would send him. His name was Adoniram Judson. He was studying at a college in America, and there were there also two or three other young men who hoped to become missionaries to the heathen.

At that time there were no missionary societies in America, and comparatively little was known of heathen lands; but in England people were beginning to know a good deal about missions. It therefore appeared the most sensible plan for one of the young men to travel to England, in order to see the gentlemen who conducted the missionary societies there. From them they would learn where it would be best to go, what money would be required, and as much about the people and country to which they were going as possible. This knowledge would prevent their wasting time in making mistakes.

Mr. Judson was chosen to go to England. I told you that this was the time of Napoleon's wars. The vessel in which he sailed was captured by a French ship, and Mr. Judson and the American sailors were shut up in its hold. Here he was very ill and very wretched; but as he could not speak French he could not explain to the doctor what was the matter, nor ask to be made more comfortable. However, the doctor saw he was a gentleman, and soon found out that he understood Latin. Then they were able to talk to each other a little.

He was taken to Bayonne, in France, and there put into a dirty prison. As he passed along the street, from the ship to the prison, he talked English quite loud and fast, in the hope that some Englishman might hear him. Happily, an American gentleman spoke to him, and told him to be quiet; and soon after he was put into prison this same gentleman came and released him.

Although he was out of prison, he was still detained in France as a prisoner-of-war; and very wisely he employed a good deal of his time in learning to speak the language. If he ever again had been put into the hold of a French vessel, I have no doubt he would have made every officer and sailor on board understand him.

Mr. Judson was, you see, imprisoned in his very first step to become a missionary. This does not appear to have disheartened him at all. He knew he should have to encounter many difficulties; but the thought hindered him from undertaking his work no more than it had hindered the apostle Paul. We read in Acts 20 that Paul went to Jerusalem, not knowing what would befall him there, only that bonds and afflictions waited for him in every city to which he went. "But," he says, "none of these things move me, neither count I my life dear unto myself, so that I might finish my course with joy, and the ministry which I have received of the Lord Jesus, to testify the gospel of the grace of God."

When at last Mr. Judson reached England, the gentlemen who superintended the affairs of the London Missionary Society gave him all the advice and help which they could, and he soon returned to America with the information that was needed. He did not remain long in America; but when he again left his native land and set sail in the ship which carried him to India, he did not go alone. A very pious young lady had consented to become his wife and to go abroad with him. She was brave as well as good. She did not know how great the troubles were which she was going to meet, but she knew that in a missionary's path there must be many difficulties. She did not fear them, for she knew Jesus was able, and had promised to help her, and she loved him. She was married to Mr. Judson only the day before the vessel sailed. Her wedding day must have been a rather sad one, she was parting from so many dear friends, and though she did not know it, she was to see them no more until they met in heaven.

Mr. and Mrs. Newell sailed in the same ship with Mr. and Mrs. Judson, and a few days after several more missionaries followed in another vessel.

Mr. and Mrs. Judson had not made up their minds in what place to settle when they left America. They intended going first to Serampore, to take the advice of the missionaries there; and they asked God to lead them to the place in which he would wish them to remain, and where he had work for them to do. They hoped this would be in India; and it would take me too long to explain why and by whom they were prevented remaining there. They went to Calcutta, but were ordered to leave the place.

After many trials and discomforts they arrived at Port Louis, in the Isle of France. Here Mrs. Newell died, and Mr. Rice, another missionary, became so ill that he returned to America. Mr. and Mrs. Judson did not think it well to remain there, and wished rather to go to Pulo Penang, Prince of Wales' Island. This was also prevented, and at last they found themselves obliged to go to Rangoon.

There were already missionaries at Rangoon, as you have heard, so that this did not seem best. Mr. Judson, too, particularly disliked the thought of going there; but as he had asked God to lead him, and had resolved to do what appeared to be God's will, he felt he should be wrong in not remaining in the place to which God had led him. God sees more than we see, and no doubt he had been preparing Mr. Judson to carry his gospel to Burmah.

The missionaries who built the mission house did not stay long in Rangoon; and very soon Mr. Judson and his wife were left alone there—two Christians in a beautiful land inhabited by millions of idolaters.

Mr. Judson, however, was not forgotten by his friends in America; when he became better known the title of doctor of divinity was conferred upon him. He did not wish for this, but he is worthy of all honor and respect, and we will in future give him his rightful title.

The mission house was built of teak boards, and was about half a mile outside the walls of the town. Though the scenery around was pretty, it could not have been a pleasant house in which to live. It was very near the place of public execution; and as the king cared more to have his own way than to make his subjects happy, a great many people were put to death there. Not far off, too, was the place where the dead were burned; for to burn instead of burying the dead is the custom of the country. Wild beasts prowled about these sad places, and by the mission house, in search of prey; and worse still, wild men followed their example, and the missionaries were never safe from robbers. This was the house in which Dr. and Mrs. Judson lived for some time after their arrival; but as soon as possible they removed into the city. The people whom they hoped to teach were in the city, not outside; and for this reason, besides many others, it was desirable to move.

CHAPTER V.

Some Visits Paid by Mrs. Judson.

DO you learn French, or German, or Latin? I dare say you do, and if you were asked: "Are these languages very easy to learn?" you would at once answer: "No; they take a great deal of time and attention, and I would often rather be at play."

Then you know something of the difficulty of our European languages; but the Burmese is far more difficult. Many French and German and Latin words are like the English, and sentences are constructed much in the same way; while the Burmese is as different as it can be: the alphabet even is quite different. Then, instead of nice, neat books like ours, the common Burmese books were made of dry palm leaves, and the words and sentences were all run into one another without any stops or divisions. When Dr. Judson studied the language there were not even grammars and dictionaries to help him, as you have; there was indeed one grammar, which had been written by a former missionary, Mr. Carey, and though there were a good many mistakes in it, it gave some assistance.

Dr. Judson, although he was clever and studied very diligently, worked hard to learn the language for several years before he considered that he knew it well enough to preach. Long before this time came, however, he could talk very well; and both he and Mrs. Judson constantly talked to any one who would listen; while by their conduct they endeavored to show the Burmese that the religion of Jesus, which they professed, was a good and holy thing.

Shall I show you how they did this?

In a poor hut, down by the river side, in dirt and misery, was lying a little child, sick and suffering. Its parents were Indians, not natives of Burmah, but like Mrs. Judson, strangers in a strange land. They were despised by the Burmese, and no one thought of helping them or their sick child. But Mrs. Judson found them out; and though it was a long, hot walk from the mission house, and she was far from strong, every day she was seen going down to the river bank to nurse and tend the babe. She loved it and its parents for Jesus' sake. I think, too, she loved it for the sake of a dear little boy of her own—a baby that God had given her for a very short time, and then taken out of her arms in that heathen land to its everlasting home in heaven.

All Mrs. Judson's love and care did not cure the poor Indian baby, though it comforted the parents. Soon this little one died as her own had done, and she and her husband saw it laid to its last rest.

Now, not far from this poor hut were residing two English sea-captains. Sometimes they watched Mrs. Judson as she walked from the mission house to the hut. They knew why she went to these poor people, and they wondered at her. They thought it strange she should care for a sick baby.

It appears to me much more strange that these two Englishmen, who might have read their Bibles every day, and who called themselves Christians, should not have better understood what Christ's religion was. Why were they not every day trying to help the many, many people who needed help? This is what Christ tells us to do; but there are still many English men and women, and children too, who care only for themselves and their own pleasure.

Soon after this Mrs. Judson herself was ill—so ill that her husband feared she would die. There was no doctor in Rangoon, and the only plan for saving her life appeared to be to send her to India, for the sake of the sea voyage and the advice of the doctors there.

So a passage was taken for her in an English vessel about to sail for Madras. When the captain heard the name of the lady passenger, and found it was Mrs. Judson who was going to Madras, he refused to take any payment from her, and said he should feel it an honor to himself and his ship to take her. Why? He was one of the two captains who had lived near the Indian huts, and there he had learned to admire Mrs. Judson, and in some degree had also learned to imitate her; for he did her a real kindness in thus saving her the expense of this journey.

Mrs. Judson returned from Madras very much improved in health. Soon after her return she paid a visit to the chief wife of the viceroy, or governor, of Rangoon. A French lady who was living in the town went with Mrs. Judson, to introduce her.

When they arrived at the government house, they were kept waiting for some time before the grand lady appeared; but the other wives of the viceroy clustered around the foreign visitors, and were much amused by the bonnets and gloves which they wore. Indeed, they took them from Mrs. Judson and her friend and tried them on. While they were thus occupied the chief wife entered, and immediately all the other women retired and sat down on the floor without speaking.

The viceroy's lady took Mrs. Judson by the hand and conducted her to a mat, on which they sat down together. She asked her visitor a great many questions about the manners of the Americans and English, and was surprised to learn that European gentlemen were not, like the Burmese, allowed to have as many wives as they pleased.

During the conversation she amused herself by ornamenting her head-dress with flowers.

While they were still talking the viceroy himself entered the room to see Mrs. Judson. He was a very savage-looking man, and wore a long robe, while in his hand he carried an enormous spear. He was, however, very polite to Mrs. Judson, and expressed pleasure at her visit. A few days before he had behaved very differently to her husband.

Mrs. Judson tried to make friends among such ladies as the viceroy's wife, with the hope that if ever her husband was persecuted for teaching the people a new religion, she might be able to obtain help for him and herself. Even savage and cruel men, you know, are sometimes persuaded to be kind by their wives.

CHAPTER VI.

Missionary Hopes and Fears in Rangoon.

DR. JUDSON had now been five years in Rangoon. He had studied hard all these years, and yet did not consider himself perfect in the difficult language. He had, however, translated the first part of the New Testament, and two or three tracts into Burmese. These had been printed at Serampore, and copies were given to any one who would receive and read them.

Mr. and Mrs. Hough had come from America to help the missionaries, so that they were no longer alone.

During these years Dr. Judson had talked to many people about the true God, and Jesus Christ his Son, whom he had sent. There had been five years of hard work, and no one as yet had embraced the religion of the gospel—no one even who had heard of it once had come again to learn more about it. Mrs. Judson had tried to teach the women, Dr. Judson had tried to teach the men, and they did not see any one yet wishing to learn. You know there is a great difference between being taught and wishing to learn.

But one day, while Dr. Judson was sitting in his house as usual, his Burmese palm-leaf books all lying about him, and his teacher sitting opposite to him, a Burman came up the steps and sat down beside him.

"How long will it take me to learn the religion of Jesus?" he asked.

How joyful Dr. Judson must have felt when he heard the question. He answered that if God gave understanding and wisdom, the religion of Jesus would be very quickly learned; but without God's help a man might study it all his life long and yet not know it.

"But how did you know anything about Jesus?" asked Dr. Judson. "I have not seen you here before."

"No," answered the Burman, "I have not been here, but I have seen two little books concerning Jesus."

"Who was Jesus?" asked Dr. Judson.

"He is the Son of God, who, pitying us, came into the world and suffered death in our stead," answered the stranger.

"And who is God?"

"He is a being without beginning or end, who is not subject to old age or death, but always is," was the answer.

Dr. Judson showed him the tracts he had translated. He recognized them at once; it was out of those little books he had learned all he knew, and he had come to the missionary with the hope that he should obtain more of that sort of writing.

Dr. Judson could only give him the first five chapters of Matthew, as that was all of the Bible yet printed in Burmese; but the man went away quite happy with his new treasure. No doubt he read many times how Jesus was born in Bethlehem of Judea in the days of Herod the king; the story of the wise men who were guided by God and the bright star to the house in which he was; of his going down into Egypt with Mary and Joseph, and then, when Herod was dead, of his coming back to Nazareth; of his baptism and temptation; his kindness to the sick and suffering; and the wonderful words of blessing and love that he spoke.

I hope he learned to love Jesus, and came back to Dr. Judson for more chapters of Matthew by-and-by, but I cannot tell you any thing more of him.

It was the year after this inquirer came to Dr. Judson, and six years after Dr. Judson came to Burmah, that he began to preach. He procured a little piece of ground in the public road leading to the chief pagoda, on which he built a small zayat—a low thatched building with open doors. A great many persons passed this zayat every day, on their way to their great pagoda, and there they could see Dr. Judson sitting on a chair, his books spread out about him, and his teacher opposite to him; or sometimes they could hear him as he read aloud parts of the tracts or of the Testament. Of course a great many people noticed him, and some would stand still and listen and wonder. Then Dr. Judson would approach them with a little Burmese tract in his hand, or a small part of the Bible, perhaps, and ask them to sit down and talk with him about this new religion which he had come to teach.

The pongyees, or Burmese priests, preach to the people in the zayats. One spring evening Dr. Judson went to a zayat to hear a Burman preach.

The room was lighted up with lamps, but instead of chairs or benches to sit upon, there were mats spread over the floor, for that is the custom of the country. There was a stand in the middle, about as high as a chair is from the ground, and when the preacher entered he seated himself here. The people were not quiet and reverent as they came in, but chattered and talked and laughed as they took their places—the men on one side and the women on the other.

"See, here come some wild foreigners," exclaimed the people, as they saw the missionaries enter. But the wild foreigners sat down upon mats, and took off their shoes. This proper behavior changed the public opinion, and the strangers were at once considered quite civilized instead of wild.

Flowers and leaves were distributed to all the persons present, and when about a hun-

A BUDDHIST SERMON.

dred were assembled, some one called for silence. It was as though they were all at school—was it not? Then every one except the missionaries took their leaves and flowers in their hands and held them above their heads, while the preacher stood up, shut his eyes, and for half an hour repeated parts of the sacred books, about the conversion of some of Gaudama's followers.

When the preacher concluded, the congregation burst into a short prayer to their false god, rose up from their mats, and went away.

This is Burmese preaching. The Burmese

have not regular sermons every week, as we have in our churches and chapels, but only now and then on special occasions.

At Dr. Judson's zayat people were coming and going all day, and sometimes he was busy talking to them one after another from morning till night. On Sundays a regular service was held and sermons were preached.

The first man who became a Christian was named Moung Nau, and very shortly after two other Burmese declared themselves disciples of Jesus. These three formed the first Christian Burmese church.

Many more were asking and thinking seriously, and Dr. Judson hoped that they would soon give up the religion of Gaudama for the religion of Jesus. He was full of hope and joy in the prospect of peace and usefulness which lay before him; and other missionaries had been sent out to help him, which made him still more happy.

But now, when all was so bright, suddenly the inquirers became afraid to be seen with the missionaries. Why was this?

A report reached Rangoon of something amiss at Ava. Some said there was a rebellion, some that the emperor was ill, some hinted that "the lord of land and water" was even dead, but they dared not say this plainly.

At length the mystery was cleared. A royal boat came down the river from Ava; the messengers who arrived in it made their way through the waiting crowds to the government house, and there they proclaimed: "Listen ye. The immortal king, wearied, it would seem, with the fatigues of royalty, has gone up to amuse himself in the celestial regions. His grandson, the heir apparent, is seated on the throne." They would not say, "The king is dead;" that would have been considered a great crime.

Well, the old king, who had now gone away "to amuse himself," had not cared to interfere much with religious affairs, and so had not molested the Christian teachers; but it was expected that the new king would not approve of the efforts they were making to convert his subjects from Buddhism.

The viceroy of Rangoon had been away from the town on an excursion of pleasure; but the very evening on which he returned he passed down the road where the mission zayat was built. He was seated upon a beautiful elephant, and was surrounded by his guards and attendants.

Dr. and Mrs. Judson were sitting in the zayat, and some Burmese were with them. The viceroy observed the little party, and noticed them very narrowly, but he passed on without making any remark. Presently two of his secretaries returned, with an order from their master, stating that he wished to see the way in which printing was done. Unfortunately, Mr. Hough, who had understood printing, had left Rangoon, and had taken the printing-press with him to Calcutta, so that the wish of the viceroy could not be gratified. He did not appear angry in consequence of this, however, and three more months passed quietly on.

At this time two persons were coming constantly to the zayat—a poor fisherman named Moung* Ing, and a learned teacher named Moung Shwagnong. Moung Ing was taught principally by Moung Nau; he soon became

* The name Moung is given to all men in Burmah while they are young; as they grow older, Moung is exchanged for Ko.

a Christian, and for many years he was a faithful helper to the missionaries.

Dr. Judson had many long and interesting conversations with Moung Shwagnong; but he was not quickly willing, like the poor fisherman, to give his heart to Jesus.

One day he was missed from his accustomed place; and a report reached Dr. Judson that he had been summoned before the viceroy, and had been accused to him of holding heretical opinions. Three weeks passed on, during which nothing more was heard of him. At the end of that time he once more appeared. He told Dr. Judson that he had not been taken before the viceroy, as was reported, but that a Mangen teacher had informed the governor that he had become a Christian. The viceroy had answered: "Inquire more about him;" and Shwagnong was so much alarmed lest more inquiries should be made, that he kept away from the zayat.

The chief pagoda of Rangoon, on the road to which the zayat was built, is called Shway Dagon. It is erected upon a rising ground two miles from the town, amid beautiful clusters of mango, cocoanut, and other tropical trees. It is considered the most sacred of the pagodas in all the country, on account of the relics of the gods preserved in it: there is the staff of Kanthathan, the water-dipper of Gaunagon, a garment of Kathapa, and, more valuable than all the rest, eight hairs of Gaudama. You do not wonder that the stone steps, with the enormous griffins on either side, are constantly trodden by worshippers who have brought offerings to the temples there. The pagoda is surrounded with temples or image-houses containing idols of Gaudama, many of them richly gilt; and close by is the large bell which every worshipper strikes after making an offering. This bell is very famous; it is so large that a man can stand upright in it, and around it is an inscription in twelve lines, about the king who presented it to the pagoda. In the year 1824 the English tried to carry this bell away, but they succeeded only in dropping it in the river; and after it had remained there for several months it was taken up by the Burmese and restored to its old place.

Dr. and Mrs. Judson were in the habit of riding along the pagoda road every morning, and of bathing in a reservoir which lay near, and which was fringed with luxuriant grass and shrubs.

One morning they were on their way to this tank as usual, when they were stopped by the same man who had accused Shwagnong to the viceroy, and were told that if ever they rode there again they should be beaten. The viceroy had given the order that no one wearing a hat, or shoes, or carrying an umbrella, or riding on a horse, should approach within the sacred grounds of Shway Dagon. This was not at all pleasant, for Dr. and Mrs. Judson were compelled to go a long way round in order to bathe; but, worse than this, it showed very plainly that the viceroy was not friendly towards the new religion or its teachers.

Dr. Judson would now sometimes sit for whole days in the zayat alone; no one came in to talk with him as formerly. Many passed by, but they did not care, or were afraid to enter.

Since the old king's death every one had been more busy than before in attending to religious duties. More pagodas were built, and more offerings of fruits and flowers, of gilt umbrellas and little flags, were presented in the temples. The great Shway Dagon itself was being regilt.

Dr. Judson feared that without the king's consent and approbation it would be of no use for him to remain at Rangoon, for he could get no listeners to his message there. He resolved, if possible, to pay a visit to Ava, and see the king himself. He purchased a boat and obtained a passport from the viceroy to go up to "the golden feet, and lift his eyes to the golden face."

Another missionary, Mr. Colman, was at Rangoon, and he accompanied Dr. Judson. They made what arrangements they could for the comfort of their wives during their absence, and with many prayers and many hopes and fears they started on their enterprise.

CHAPTER VII.

VISITS TO THE KING AT AVA, AND THEIR RESULTS.

IT was just at Christmas time that Dr. Judson and Mr. Colman left Rangoon on this journey to Ava. Not cold Christmas, with snow whitening the landscape, and icicles hanging from the bare branches of the trees. Such Christmases are not known in Burmah. The banks of the river were green with the foliage of the trees; the sun was shining warm overhead, and the missionaries were glad of shelter from its rays.

They embarked in a long boat; it was forty feet long, but not very wide, and as there were in all eighteen persons on board, and there were no cabins, it must have been a little crowded. There were ten rowers, a steersman, a headman—who, I suppose, was responsible for the good behavior of the others—a cook, a dhobee, or washerman, and an Englishman who wished to go to the capital to offer his services to the king.

Two little rooms had been constructed on the boat with bamboos and mats and palm-leaf thatch; in these the missionaries could just sit or lie down.

Moung Nau, of whom you heard in the last chapter, went as cook and steward; and the Englishman took care of the guns, which they were obliged to have on account of the robbers who infested the banks of the river.

Besides all these the boat carried several pieces of fine cloth and other articles intended as presents, and especially a present for the king. This was a beautiful large copy of the English Bible, in six volumes, every volume bound in a gilt cover, and wrapped in handsome cloth. Dr. Judson would have been glad to take it to the king in his own language, so that he might read it, but it was not yet translated.

Copies of the tracts that he had translated, and of the New Testament, as far as it was completed, Dr. Judson had with him; and he hoped to find many opportunities of giving them to persons who might read them.

Shwagnong had been asked by the missionaries to accompany them, but he declined. However, he came down to the wharf to see the boat start, and when he had bidden adieu to his friends, he stood looking after them until they passed out of sight in a bend of the river.

Away went the boat up the river. Happily it was nowhere attacked by robbers, though it passed places where other boats had been attacked only a few days before. At one town, Kahnoung, the travellers met an officer, with a party of men, who was going in pursuit of a band of robbers that had attacked a large boat, wounded a good many of the men, and stolen all the property on board. This officer offered to go with the missionaries through a dangerous part of the river lying before them. Dr. Judson, however, could not afford the presents he and his men would expect; and this did not trouble him, for he knew he had a stronger and wiser guardian in his heavenly Father.

On the boat went, up the broad river: past

peopled towns, whose pagodas glittered in the sunlight; past scattered villages; past forests and jungles and rice-plains; past ruined cities, where kings had once dwelt, and busy crowds had once moved to and fro attending to their daily tasks, or carrying offerings to their heathen temples; and at last, after five weeks' journeying, the missionaries reached Ava.

They called upon a former governor of Rangoon, and were very politely received by him. Dr. Judson presented both the governor and his wife with handsome presents, and received through him an introduction to Moung Zah, a private minister of state, called an a-tween-woon. This minister had the power of presenting them to the king.

The very next day after their arrival they went to the palace to see Moung Zah. They carried with them the Bible for the king, and other presents for the ministers. After they had satisfied the officers at the gates that they were expected, they were allowed to pass; and having given a present for Moung Zah to his servants, they were conducted to his apartments.

The minister received them very pleasantly; he expected his visitors, and perhaps was pleased with his present. He told the missionaries to sit down before some governors who were with him, and inquired who they were, and for what purpose they were come. He heard that they had come to the country with the hope of teaching the people a new religion, and that they wished to present to the king a petition and their sacred books. Moung Zah then asked some questions about God, and looked at the petition.

Just then some one announced that "the golden foot was about to advance." Moung Zah rose at once and put on his state robes. Then he turned to Dr. Judson and Mr. Colman, and said: "How can you hope to spread your religion in this empire? But come along." He evidently did not think that the king would allow his people to become Christians if he could help it; and it was with rather heavy hearts that the missionaries followed him.

It was a very grand day at the palace. Large numbers of people were assembled, and there was a great deal of parade and show, for a great victory was being celebrated.

Moung Zah led the missionaries up a large flight of stairs into a magnificent hall. It was very high and very wide, with many large pillars supporting the roof and beautiful dome. Every part of this spacious hall was completely covered with gold, like the temple which Solomon built in Jerusalem. There were not many people in the hall, but they were evidently very important, and were waiting for the king.

After they had waited about five minutes, Moung Zah whispered that the king had entered. From their position it was not possible to see the farther end of the hall, but the missionaries leaned as far forward as possible, in order to obtain a view of his majesty. Every one laid his head in the dust as the king approached. He came alone, carrying in his hand a sword in a golden sheath.

Dr. Judson and Mr. Colman did not lie down on the ground as the Burmese did. They remained kneeling, with their hands folded, and looked straight at the king. He looked at them, then he stopped, and asked:

"Who are these?"

"The teachers, great king," said Dr. Judson.

"What! you speak Burmese? You are the priests I heard of last night. When did you arrive? Are you teachers of religion? Are you married? Why do you dress so?"

Dr. Judson answered these questions, and the king appeared pleased. He sat down on a high seat, with his hand resting upon the hilt of his sword, to hear the petition which Moung Zah read; it was as follows:

"The American teachers present themselves to receive the favor of the excellent king, the sovereign of land and sea.

"Hearing that, on account of the greatness of the royal power, the royal country was in a quiet and prosperous state, we arrived at the town of Rangoon, within the royal dominions, and having obtained leave of the governor of that town to come up and behold the golden face, we have ascended and reached the bottom of the golden feet.

"In the great country of America we sustain the character of teachers and explainers of the contents of the sacred Scriptures of our religion. And since it is contained in those Scriptures that, if we pass to other countries, and preach and propagate religion, great good will result, and both those who teach and those who receive the religion will be freed from future punishment, and enjoy, without decay or death, the eternal happiness of heaven — that royal permission be given that we, taking refuge in the royal power, may preach our religion in these dominions, and that those who are pleased with our preaching, and wish to listen to and be guided by it, whether foreigners or Burmese, may be exempt from government molestation, they present themselves to receive the favor of the excellent king, the sovereign of land and sea."

The king listened while Moung Zah read; then he took the petition and read it all through to himself. He handed it back without saying one word, and took a tract which Moung Zah presented.

The missionaries' hearts were lifted to God; they hoped and prayed for Burmah. The king read the first two sentences of the tract, and then he dashed it to the ground. He would not even look at the fine gilt-covered copy of the Bible, but rose from his seat, strode to the other end of the hall, which was open, and there threw himself upon a cushion, to listen to the music and watch the show of elephants and soldiers outside.

If the Burmese believed in Jesus, it must be without the permission of their king. Indeed, from what had happened in Ava in years gone by, it was evident that if any one became a Christian, now that the king had refused his consent, they could expect only persecution and death. Fifteen years before this, a young Burman had become a Roman-catholic, and had been frightfully beaten with an iron club, on account of his religion. After that, the Roman-catholic priests had left off trying to convert the Burmese, and had only attended to foreigners.

It was the fear of such treatment from their rulers as this Burman had received, that had alarmed the Christians and inquirers at Rangoon; and it was to save them from such fear that Dr. Judson had undertaken this journey to Ava. But the attempt had been unsuccessful; and now, as Dr. Judson glided down the Irrawadi in his boat, from Ava back to Rangoon, he feared that he should be obliged to give up preaching Christ in Burmah, for he thought no one would venture to listen to him.

On the Sunday after he reached Rangoon, when the three converts were with him, secretly, in the evening, he told them of all that had occurred at Ava, and how, if they remained in Rangoon, they would certainly be persecuted.

He told them he thought of removing to Chittagong, a place which is under the Bengal government; and he asked them whether they would go also.

Two of them, Moung Nau and Moung Thahlah, said they would go; but the third, Moung Bya, could not leave Burmah, for he had a wife in Rangoon, and no Burmese woman is allowed to leave the country. Moung Bya, however, loved the missionaries and what they had taught him so much, that he did not at all like the thought of losing his teachers. Besides, he felt that Dr. Judson was making a mistake in intending to leave the town.

A few days after, Moung Bya came again

to the mission house, accompanied by his brother-in-law, Moung Myat-yah.

"I have come," said Moung Bya, "to ask you not to leave Rangoon at present."

"I think," replied Dr. Judson, "that it is of no use for me to remain here. I cannot open the zayat; no Burman will venture to examine the religion I teach, and so no one will believe it."

"Teacher," said Moung Bya, "my mind is distressed; I cannot eat or sleep, since you are going away. I have been among those who live near us, and I find even now some are secretly examining the new religion. My brother, Myat-yah, is one of them. Do stay with us a few months. Stay until there are eight or ten Christians here, and then, even if you leave the country, the religion will spread of itself—the king cannot stop it."

I think Moung Bya was right. "Let us all," he said, "make an effort; as for me, I will pray."

Dr. Judson felt he could not leave; for one and another and another came, as Moung Bya had come, begging him to remain and continue to teach them. In spite of the fear of persecution, and though the zayat was closed, he found the people were willing to listen privately, and many were longing to learn about Jesus, who could save them from their sins.

He resolved to remain, for evidently, notwithstanding the king, God had work for him to do in that city. Mr. and Mrs. Colman, however, went to Chittagong, with the hope of making a station to which other missionaries might go, or to which the Christians at Rangoon might flee if they should be forced to leave Burmah.

In a short time there were not only ten, but eighteen Burmese Christians in Rangoon. Neither the king nor the viceroy interfered to persecute the missionaries or their converts; and Dr. Judson was once more filled with thankfulness and hope.

He was obliged, however, to part for a time with his dear wife; for Mrs. Judson became so ill that she was obliged to take a long sea voyage, and went first to England and then to America, for the sake of her health. How glad she must have been to see her dear friends in America once more! and with what pleasure they must have listened to all the interesting details of her life in Burmah!

While Mrs. Judson was absent, Dr. Price and Mr. and Mrs. Hough arrived at Rangoon to assist Dr. Judson.

Dr. Price was a medical doctor, and as soon as the king heard of his arrival, he sent for him to come to Ava. As Dr. Price did not yet understand the language, Dr. Judson went to Ava with him in order to interpret for him.

The king did not seem to remember that he had ever before seen Dr. Judson; for one day, when he was interpreting for Dr. Price, the king turned to him, and said:

"And you in black, who are you?"

"A teacher of religion, your majesty."

But his majesty was very gracious, and even told Dr. Judson that he might have some land to build a house in Ava, and that he should like both the missionaries to remain in the city.

This was very different treatment from that which Dr. Judson had received the first time he visited Ava; but no doubt it was because the king hoped to get some good from the medicines Dr. Price could give him, and not because he cared for Dr. Judson or the religion he taught.

Dr. Judson returned to Rangoon to meet his wife. As soon as she arrived he intended removing to Ava. The little church at Rangoon could be left now to the care of the new missionaries; and he hoped in a short time to form another church in the capital city itself.

The translation of the New Testament had been progressing during all these years, and while Dr. Judson was waiting at Rangoon for his wife he completed this work. It was not yet a printed book, but it was all written upon paper ready to be printed—the precious story of our Saviour's life and death; of his resurrection and ascension, the account of his apostles' travels and sufferings; the letters they wrote; down to the last words that Jesus gave us to remember: "Behold, I come quickly; blessed is he that keepeth the sayings of the prophecy of this book."

CHAPTER VIII.

DR. JUDSON AND DR. PRICE IN THE PRISON.

IN this chapter you will not hear of missionary work, but of cruel imprisonment and bitter suffering.

Mrs. Judson reached Rangoon safely, and in much better health than when she left. She found her husband waiting for her, in order to take her with him to Ava, and it was not long before they started.

On their way up the river they often landed at the villages; and to the dark villagers a white woman was quite a curiosity. They would make remarks to each other about Mrs. Judson, and then run on in front, so as to have a good long stare as she came up.

Not very far from Ava they saw upon the river a fleet of boats. They were war-boats, adorned with gold, and filled with Burmese soldiers. The soldiers were on their way to fight against the English at Chittagong, and at their head was their great general, Bandoola.

Bandoola ordered Dr. Judson's boat to be stopped and examined—that was not at all pleasant. However, the missionaries were allowed to pass on, and they reached the end of their journey in safety.

When Dr. and Mrs. Judson met that fleet of war-ships, they little knew what sad trouble the war would bring to them.

Dr. Price met them at Ava, and in a fortnight's time they had built a little board house to live in. It contained three rooms and a verandah, and was raised by stakes four feet from the ground. A fortnight seems a very short time for building a house, does it not? but this is a very common kind of dwelling in Burmah. They hoped in time to have a better—a brick house, which would not so quickly get heated through by the sun. Mrs. Judson says this little board house was like an oven.

Dr. Judson began at once to teach and preach, and Mrs. Judson was busy with some little girls, who had been brought to her by their father, that she might teach them. She called them Mary and Abby.

The king was not in Ava when Dr. and Mrs. Judson arrived, but he soon returned, accompanied by all his viceroys and officers, dressed in their most splendid robes. They entered the city, mounted on enormous elephants and handsome horses, making a very fine procession; and the white elephant, adorned with gold and jewels, was a most beautiful object.

There was peace and rejoicing in Ava; but many war-boats constantly went down the river, and Mrs. Judson could watch them as they passed her house, and see how smart and joyful the soldiers looked, who were going, as they believed, to conquer the English.

The English fleet had sailed up the river to Rangoon; but the king expected that the ships would soon be driven back, and that all the English soldiers and sailors would be killed or taken prisoners. So firmly did he believe this, that he gave orders to his officers not to kill them all, but to keep some for slaves, and to be especially careful to preserve guns and ammunition, as they would be useful when next he went to war with the Siamese. The

Burmese knew that the English had conquered the Hindoos, but this did not alarm them; they considered themselves a vastly superior nation, and supposed that the English had never yet fought with a people so brave as themselves, nor with any as skilful in the use of the sword and spear.

Dr. and Mrs. Judson hoped, as they were Americans, and not English, that, in spite of the war, they would not be interfered with, but would be allowed to continue their work in security.

In this they were disappointed. The Burmese knew so little of geography and history that they thought all white men, except the French, were subjects of Britain; and that, since the overthrow of Napoleon at the battle of Waterloo, even France had become part of the English dominions. Dr. and Mrs. Judson spoke the English language, and received their money through Englishmen; so no wonder the Burmese did not believe them when they said they belonged to a different nation.

One day, just as dinner was ready in the mission house, a Burmese officer and some men rushed into the room, and with them one

ARREST OF DR. JUDSON.

who had a ring tattooed on his face. He was an executioner from the prison.

Dr. Judson was seized and thrown on the floor; ropes were tied tightly round his wrists, and he was dragged away to prison. The cords were tied so tightly round his arms that they cut through the flesh; but this was only the beginning of cruelties. Almost all his clothes were stripped off him, and every thing that he had in his pockets was taken away.

In the middle of the prison-yard he was made to sit down. Here a block of stone was placed, and on this block a smith, with a maul, fixed upon his ankles three pairs of fetters. He was bid to get up and walk into the prison house. The chains were heavy, and they fastened his feet so closely together, that it was with difficulty he could move at all. But the wicket of the prison house was at length reached and closed upon him.

If I tell you something of what the prison room was like, you will perhaps understand a little of the misery that Dr. Judson, a Christian gentleman, who loved cleanliness and neatness, must have endured there.

The room into which Dr. Judson was locked was called the Let-ma-yoon-toung, or death prison; because almost all imprisoned there were, sooner or later, put to death.

It was built of strong teak boards, without windows, or indeed any regular opening except the doorway. Happily, the boards did not join very neatly, and there were chinks and crevices through which a little light and air found entrance; or how could the forty or fifty prisoners, who lay in chains upon the floor, have existed at all?

In the centre of the room was a tripod, on which stood an earthenware oil lamp. The only other furniture consisted of stocks; and many of the poor creatures, besides wearing chains, had their feet fast in the stocks.

Dr. Price, and all the other white men in Ava, were brought to this terrible prison. But, though they were there together, they were not allowed to speak to each other in their own languages, lest they should say something they did not wish their jailers to hear.

When night came the white prisoners were made to lie down in a row upon the bare and dirty floor; and there they were strung together by a long bamboo passed between their chained legs. The bamboo was then hoisted from the ground by pulleys and ropes at each end, until half of their bodies was raised from the floor; and when the jailer had in this way made them as uncomfortable as possible, he wished them "good night," and left them.

The first night in that prison must have been very terrible. Besides the misery of lying on such a dirty floor, and in such a very uncomfortable position, there was to be endured the pain caused by the heavy fetters, by the swollen and bleeding wrists; and all around there was the sight of others in pain and misery also.

Then, too, there was the thought of those outside. What had happened to the dear wife from whom Dr. Judson had been so cruelly separated? She was left alone among the wicked, heartless people. She might already be dead, or she might soon be brought to join him in the prison.

Morning dawned, and through the crevices of the walls streamed in rays of light, which told the prisoners of the glad sunshine God was pouring over the earth. But though his servants in the prison were shut out from the full sunlight, they were not shut out of God's sight, nor from the light of his countenance.

With the morning came the jailer, to count over his prisoners and to see that none had escaped. Do you expect to hear that breakfast came too? Nothing of the kind. No food was supplied to the prisoners, unless a friend brought them a meal, or some charitable person remembered them and sent a supply of boiled rice. So it came to pass that those who had not friends often died of starvation, and those who were not regularly supplied looked haggard and thin, and when they did get a meal, they often ate so much as to make themselves ill.

The day wore on. There were groans and curses to be heard; there were pain and agony to be witnessed and endured through the long, weary hours.

Afternoon came; it was nearly three o'clock. Why was every one becoming silent, and looking so frightened? The gong sounded the hour; the wicket opened; in walked one of the spotted executioners, and without a word, he seized a prisoner and carried him away for execution. It was always at three o'clock that the executioner entered, if any one was to be put to death that day. Do you wonder that all grew silent and fearful as the dread hour approached, since no one knew who would be taken next?

Mrs. Judson did not come to inquire for her husband for three days. She had not been put in prison, but she had been guarded in her house; all her boxes had been searched, and a good deal of money taken from her.

She had thought it better at once to destroy all her letters and papers—all except the precious manuscript of the New Testament. This she did not destroy, but to preserve it, she fastened it up in a piece of common cotton cloth, and wound a mat round it to make a pillow.

When, at the end of three days, Mrs. Judson was permitted to leave her house, she went at once to the prison. Her husband was allowed to creep out into the court to receive her. How shocked she must have been to see him in such a condition. How sad their meeting was!

Mrs. Judson, however, was not a lady who wasted time in grieving when it was possible to make things better. She tried to comfort and cheer her husband, and instead of going home to weep, she made herself busy in preparing food, and clean clothing, and pillows, not only for Dr. Judson, but for the other white prisoners also.

You can guess what pillow was carried to Dr. Judson. No one but he and his wife, and the God who rules all things, knew how precious that pillow was.

The white prisoners in the dreadful death prison had not been left without food during those three days, for some of the native servants had remembered their masters, and brought them their meals. Through all the eighteen months of their imprisonment this was done.

Mrs. Judson went from governor to governor, hoping to find one among them who would take compassion upon her, and her husband, and the white prisoners; but she met only with unkindness. At length, by bribes, she induced the governor of the prison to allow them to come out of the loathsome room to a corner of an open shed opposite the prison door. Here they stayed for a few days, and were even provided with water to wash themselves.

That governor of the jail appears to have been really sorry for Mrs. Judson, and to have been willing to help her when he could; but he dared not do much. She was, however, allowed to come frequently to the prison court, and to talk sometimes with her husband. How she must have longed to unfasten the cruel chains around his ankles, and to dress the wounds on his wrists which the tight cords had made!

In the midst of all this trouble God sent a baby girl to Mrs. Judson. Poor little baby! It was sent into a sad home. Its mother carried it to the prison when it was only two or three weeks old, and there its father first saw and kissed his little Maria.

Mrs. Judson had now plenty to do; for, besides her baby to nurse and tend, there were Mary and Abby to be thought for at home, and her husband in the prison to see and comfort; there was his food, too, to prepare and carry; and besides attending to all this, she constantly endeavored to obtain favors for him from one governor or another.

Mrs. Judson had more to do than she was strong enough to accomplish; but to Dr. Judson in that dreary, dirty prison, the hours must have worn away very, very slowly. The fetters were not taken off; but after a time the jailers became less strict about the speaking, and the white prisoners did sometimes manage to say a few words to each other.

Dr. Judson and another gentleman, Mr. Gouger, contrived a chess-board between them, by means of which they whiled away many weary hours. An old piece of buffalo skin was the board; the squares were marked out with real lampblack, for they obtained it from the lamp which burned always in the middle of the room; and from a bit of bamboo, with a knife, they cut out some men which, though not very handsome, answered the purpose well enough.

Some of the prisoners were, no doubt, very wicked men; there were thieves and murderers among them, but some appear to have done nothing worthy of so unhappy a fate, and some seem to have been quite out of their minds.

One prisoner was accused of having made an image of the king, and then of walking over it. I suppose this was considered a very great insult to his majesty. One night the inhuman jailers killed the poor man who committed this crime by breaking his spine.

Another man had said he could fly, and so he was put in prison. He must have been out of his mind. In this country he would have been taken to a comfortable asylum, where he would have had a doctor to attend to him, and every thing about him made as cheerful and comfortable as possible, with the hope that when he was comfortable and happy his mind might get better. In Burmah he was taken to the Let-ma-yoon-toung; and the jailers were so afraid lest he really should fly away that they took extraordinary pains to keep him fast. Three pairs of irons were fastened round his ankles, and his feet were put in the stocks. His wrists were bound together with a long rope, and the other end was tied to a rafter in the ceiling. His long hair was twisted into braids, and each braid was pinned to the floor, and a rope round his waist was also fastened to the floor.

You will say that now he certainly could not fly away. The jailers were not quite so certain, and the poor lunatic still said he would. One more thing they could still do to secure him. They passed cords through the holes bored in his ears for rings, and pinned them also to the ground.

One day there was a cry of fire in the city. Two or three of the executioners ran out immediately, for there would certainly be work for them. By-and-by they returned, leading a man who had his hands tied behind him, his face smeared with charcoal, and a firebrand hanging round his neck. The unfortunate man had carelessly set fire to his house. The next day he was whipped through the streets, and then released.

As so many of the houses were built of wood, and one being carelessly set on fire might have caused a very great deal of mischief, this man deserved some punishment. People ought to be very thoughtful when, by want of care, they may cause loss, or danger, or even discomfort to others.

Through the entreaties of Mrs. Judson the white prisoners had been again allowed to leave the inner prison, and to occupy some of the little cells around the courtyard.

They had been imprisoned for some months, when one day—it was on the first of March—came the intelligence that the Burmese troops had been defeated, and that the English army, instead of being driven back, was advancing up the river to Prome.

When this news reached Ava the white prisoners were, one by one, brought from their cells and assembled in silence round the block of stone in the centre of the court. Here two more pairs of fetters were fixed upon their legs, and then, hardly able to move, they were sent again into the prison.

This took place when little Maria was about two months old. Mrs. Judson does not seem to have gone to the prison herself that day; but her husband sent her word of what had happened, and that his mat and pillow, and all that he had, had been taken away by his jailers.

The loss of the pillow was, as you know, a very serious matter.

Mrs. Judson found out as soon as possible which of the men had taken possession of the precious pillow, and gave him in exchange one much handsomer and better looking. I dare say he wondered why she cared to have that old cotton pillow; it looked worth almost nothing, and was very hard. He could not guess what a treasure it contained, and how much labor and thought were rolled up in that worthless-looking thing.

The Let-ma-yoon-toung was at this time very full. A number of prisoners-of-war were confined there, so that nearly a hundred men were shut up in that close room. It was the hot season too. Soon the white men were so ill that it was really a great wonder they did not all die.

Mrs. Judson went many times to the governor of the jail, begging that they might be released, or at any rate be made more comfortable. No doubt they owed their lives to her exertions. The governor of the prison once said to her with tears in his eyes:

"I pity you; and, believe me, I do not wish to increase the sufferings of the prisoners. Three times the queen's brother has desired me to assassinate them privately, but I would not. I will never execute your husband; but I cannot release him—you must not ask me."

The governor, however, allowed them to

drag themselves every day to the prison-door, there to receive and eat their dinner; and this daily refreshment, little as it was, must have been a great comfort.

For a long time Mrs. Judson contrived to convey little notes to her husband. They were generally hidden in the dish on which his meals were carried to him; sometimes the spout of a coffee-pot was stuffed with a little roll of paper; and in these notes she told him many things which she was afraid of saying aloud. At last these notes were discovered, and Mrs. Judson very narrowly escaped being imprisoned also. Perhaps her friend the governor saved her from this.

At the end of March the Burmese gained a victory over the English at Ramoo. When the news of this triumph reached Ava it caused great rejoicing. Some English prisoners had been taken by Bandoola; and these prisoners, with the baggage, arms, and ammunition which had been captured, were paraded through the city in a public procession, which the king came out to see.

Soon after this victory the Burmese general, Bandoola, was killed by the explosion of a bombshell; and his troops were so discouraged in consequence that they were quite afraid to fight. I think Bandoola's death frightened the king also ; but he showed his alarm in a strange way. The messenger who brought the intelligence was the general's own brother; and the king at once ordered that his head should be cut off.

CHAPTER IX.

THE PRISON AT DUNG-BEN-LAI.

ANOTHER month passed away, and in May the white prisoners were once more assembled round the stone block in the court. There they stood, a haggard, dirty, hollow-eyed, miserable group; not this time to have their fetters fastened on, but to have all taken off.

What! were they free?

No, indeed, far from that. Their fetters were knocked off, and then they were tied together two and two, and led out of the prison court along the street. They believed they were all to be killed, for they were going towards the place of execution. Presently, however, the jailers turned down another road, and soon they were out of the town, walking at midday over a plain of burning sand. Burning, indeed, it must have been to their bare feet and under that tropical sun. Their feet were very tender, they had so long been unaccustomed to walking; soon blisters formed upon the soles, and burst and bled. They were weary and sick and faint, and yet in spite of pain and exhaustion they were still driven on by their jailers.

One man, a Greek, dropped down upon the road and died; and Dr. Judson was so ill and weak that he would have done the same, had not a servant run up just in time. This kind man took off his turban, tore it up, and with it bound up Dr. Judson's bleeding feet; then for the rest of the day he walked by his side and helped him along.

The second day the journey was continued in a cart; for so stiff and sore were all the prisoners that even the jailers saw it was impossible for them to walk. By the evening they reached Oung-ben-lai, the place at which they were to stop.

The prison at Oung-ben-lai was not considered very secure, and therefore the prisoners were made fast in the stocks. The stocks, too, were hoisted off the ground, as had been done at the Let-ma-yoon-toung. The place swarmed with mosquitoes, and these troublesome insects settled thickly upon their sore feet; they could not reach them with their hands to drive them away, and the pain and irritation were terrible. They made so much noise that at last the jailer came and lowered the stocks, and after that the weary men obtained a little rest.

The morning that the white prisoners were so suddenly removed from the Let-ma-yoon-toung, Mrs. Judson had been as usual with her husband. While they were talking together, the governor of the jail sent a messenger to say he wished to see her immediately. She went to him at once, and found he only wanted to ask some questions about his watch, which, he said, was not keeping good time. She wished to hasten back to her husband, but he detained her as long as possible.

At last she left him and returned to the jail. But where was her husband? Where was Dr. Price? Where were all the white prisoners? Gone, gone; and no one could tell her where. She hurried along the streets with her baby in her arms, asking all she met if they had seen the white prisoners. At length she heard that they had been taken away out of the town in the direction of Oung-ben-lai. It was a relief to hear this, for she had greatly feared that they had been taken to execution, and that she should never see her husband more.

She returned to the governor to learn the truth, but he told her he knew nothing more than she had already heard. He too seemed to have believed that they would be put to death, for he kindly said: "I will send off a man to follow them, and see, what is to be done. You can do nothing more for your husband; take care of yourself."

But Mrs. Judson felt she could not take care of herself; she must follow her husband, whatever happened. She knew that, marching through the day under that scorching sun, without even an umbrella to shelter him, he would surely be ill; and if she were not by him, there would be no one to bring him nourishment or to comfort him.

The next morning she left Ava to follow the prisoners to Oung-ben-lai, with Koochil the cook, little Mary and Abby, and her baby Maria lying on her bosom. Part of the way they went in a boat up the river, and part of the way in a cart.

The precious pillow was safe. It had been thrown away in the jail court as rubbish. But Moung Ing had been there in the course of the day; he happened to see it, and as it had belonged to his master, and he knew that for some reason it was valued, he carried it away to Mrs. Judson. I do not think he knew what was in it; but doubtless it was the great and good God who directed Moung Ing's eyes to it, and put the thought in his heart to keep it.

Mrs. Judson reached Oung-ben-lai the day after her husband. It was a rising ground surrounded with vast rice plains. The prison itself was a much more airy house than that at Ava, and in this respect it was better; but the prison and the land around was infested with serpents and other creatures nearly as bad. When the rice plantations were inundated, large numbers of animals took refuge from the waters on this rising ground. All the prisoners were allowed to arm themselves with large sticks, in order to defend themselves; and during the time that they remained there they killed more than a dozen cobra-capellos, which are, you know, very poisonous serpents, and great numbers that were less dangerous.

When the prisoners arrived at their new prison they noticed that in the space between the floor and the ground there were piled large numbers of fagots. Did the king intend to have the house and prisoners all burnt together? Was this what the governor meant when he said: "Take care of yourself; you can do nothing more for your husband?" It may have been the case; but if so, God turned his heart and saved Dr. Judson and his friends.

One day a new prisoner came to Oung-ben-lai. A strange prisoner, indeed! A lion in his cage. It is quite possible that the king intended him to eat up the white captives. No reason was given for his coming. He was a fine Arabian lion, which had been sent as a present to the king. No food was given to the poor animal; he was left, as many other prisoners had been left, to die of starvation. The poor lion roared terribly, and dashed itself against the strong bars of its cage so fiercely that it was soon wounded and bleeding.

Sometimes a kind woman would give it a piece of meat; but this was not enough to satisfy it, only enough to make it long for more, so that the kindness only made matters worse. Sometimes one of the jailers would fling pails of water over the poor beast's heated skin. This would make it shriek with pleasure; but it wanted a supply of food, which it could not get, and day by day it grew weaker and weaker until it died. Then its body was dragged out of its cage and buried.

Why had this strange prisoner been sent to Oung-ben-lai? I cannot tell. Some thought that the king really had intended that the white prisoners should have been given to it as food. It was far better that it should die of starvation than that it should eat them. Some thought there was another reason. The lion had been a great favorite; but it was whispered in Ava that this conquering English people had upon their standard the representation of a lion. Is it possible the king was foolish enough to think that if his lion died the people with the lion standard might be overcome? The jailer as he watched the poor creature's struggles would sometimes say that it was the British lion in vain trying to struggle against the Burmese. Whatever was the reason, the poor lion at Oung-ben-lai died; but those who fought under the English standard were bold and brave and conquering still.

At this time Dr. Judson was lying weak and ill with fever; and the day after the lion's death, as he dragged his chains with difficulty to the doorway, to meet his wife and kiss his baby daughter, he begged her to try and obtain permission for him to lie in the empty lion's cage, instead of in the terrible prison. The jailer gave permission. Mrs. Judson made the cage as clean as she could for her husband, and then he took possession of it thankfully. Here he had more air than in the prison, and soon recovered a little from his fever.

Mrs. Judson was near her husband at Oung-ben-lai, but her troubles seemed to grow worse and worse. She asked permission to put up a little bamboo house near the prison. This was not allowed, but one of the jailers took her to his house. There were in it only two tiny dirty rooms; one of these two he and his family occupied, and in the other Mrs. Judson, with Koochil and the children, lived for six months.

There was great difficulty in procuring food, even of the coarsest kind. A llttle rice or dried fish was all that could be obtained, and sometimes not even that.

The very day after their arrival Mary took the smallpox, and then little Maria sickened with it. Mrs. Judson had to tend them besides her suffering husband. Soon she was ill too, so ill that she could with difficulty crawl to the prison. Weak as she was, she set off in a cart to Ava to procure medicines, which she had left there, and to buy better food. When she returned, so weak and altered was she, that, as she crawled into the room again, Koochil burst into tears at the sight of his mistress.

For two months she could not get up from the mat which was her only bed, and what she would have done without the good and kind Koochil, I do not know. He waited upon his mistress and the children; he brought wood for the fire and water to boil the rice.

BEGGING MILK FOR THE BABE.

He prepared and carried Dr. Judson's meals, and was often so busy all day long that he had no time to eat any thing himself until night. He asked for no wages, for he knew his mistress could hardly find money to buy food; he worked and waited and hoped for better days—he was serving God as well as his master and mistress. Dr. and Mrs. Judson loved him, and rewarded him when the better days dawned. I am sure God, too, loved and rewarded him.

Poor little Maria was perhaps worse off than any one just now when Mrs. Judson was ill; a baby needs milk, and her mother could neither give her any, nor buy it, for there was none to be bought. So baby was nearly starved, and cried constantly. She would certainly have died, had not the jailers allowed Dr. Judson to come out of prison for a few hours every day, in order to carry her round the village and beg the mothers of babies to spare a little milk for her. In this way the poor little child was kept alive.

These days were very, very dark indeed; but brighter ones were coming.

When Dr. Judson had been a prisoner for a year and a half, he was removed from Oung-ben-lai. He was not yet made a free man, but he was wanted by the king as interpreter. The king wished to make peace with the English, and a good deal of talking and writing had to be done before all the arrangements could be made. Dr. Price was also wanted; and by-and-by, when peace was finally arranged, they, and all the other white prisoners, were made free.

Mrs. Judson returned to Ava when her husband left Oung-ben-lai. There she was again taken very ill—it seemed hardly possible she should recover. Her husband was away upon the king's business. He did not know how ill she was; and had he known, he could not have come to her. He was even brought to Ava, and passed by the door of the house where his wife was lying, but was not allowed to enter. He was still a prisoner.

But the next morning the governor who had so often befriended him set Dr. Judson free, with permission to go home.

He hurried along the streets; the door of his house was open; he entered. A dirty, fat, half-naked woman was squatting on the floor by a little fire. In her arms was a poor, neglected baby—one so dirty that Dr. Judson did not for a moment imagine it was his little Maria. But what were the woman and child doing in his house?

He hastened into the next room to find his wife. He found her lying across the foot of the bed, asleep. But how altered every thing was! How pale and thin and wasted she was! how dirty and uncomfortable the room in which she lay! No doubt Koochil had done his very best; but he could not properly nurse a sick lady and a baby.

For many days Mrs. Judson had known nothing of what was passing around her, and so could not direct her willing servant. At one time some Burmese neighbors had entered the room to see her die. "She is dead," they said; "and if the King of angels should come in, he could not recover her."

But they were wrong. The King of angels was there, and he restored her for a little while to her husband and child. Now that her husband was at liberty she had a better nurse; and in the joy of being together again, free, after this sad, sad time, how happy they must have been!

It was, of course, not desirable to remain at

Ava. As soon as Mrs. Judson was well enough they went to the English camp at Yandabo. Dr. Judson speaks of that journey down the Irrawadi as quite delicious after the long months of imprisonment. He says: "What

do you think of floating down the Irrawadi, on a cool, moonlight evening, with your wife by your side, and your baby in your arms? Free—all free! I can never regret my twenty-one months of misery when I recall that one delicious thrill. I think I have had a better appreciation of what heaven may be ever since."

Sir Archibald Campbell, the English general, was at Yandabo, and a great many Burmese governors had assembled there to arrange the peace. Sir Archibald Campbell gave them all a dinner soon after Dr. and Mrs. Judson arrived. It was a very grand dinner in a tent; there were flags flying and bands playing. When the dinner hour arrived, the company rose two and two to take their places, but Sir Archibald walked before them alone. They reached the tent; the music stopped, and every one stood still. This surprised the Burmese; they wondered what would happen next. The general went into the tent, and soon appeared leading Mrs. Judson, whom he placed by his side at the head of the table. All the guests took their seats; but the Burmese governors looked very uncomfortable. There was not one of them who had not been unkind to Mrs. Judson, and they saw that now it was in her power to treat them as they had treated her.

The general soon noticed the looks of his

guests. He turned to Mrs. Judson, and said: "I think these gentlemen must be acquaintances of yours, and judging from their looks, you must have used them very ill."

Mrs. Judson only smiled; but the Burmese saw that the general was speaking of them, though they could not understand English, and they became more and more frightened.

"What is the matter with that man with a pointed beard?" continued Sir Archibald; "he seems to be seized with an ague fit."

"I cannot tell," answered Mrs. Judson, "unless his memory is busy. He is an old acquaintance of mine, and perhaps may infer danger to himself from seeing me under your protection." She then went on to tell the general why this guest was so afraid. At the time Dr. Judson was confined in the inner prison, ill with fever, and with five pairs of fetters on, she had walked several miles to beg a favor of this man. She was worn and very thin in consequence of illness and sorrow; but in spite of her weakness and the great heat, she had taken her umbrella and, for her husband's sake, had gone to ask for what she wanted. The governor had refused her request; but as she turned away from his door, weary and downcast, he noticed her nice silk umbrella, and without ceremony or apology, he seized it. She begged him to return it, as it was dangerous to walk in the sun without some protection; but he would not listen. She begged him at least to give her in exchange a common paper umbrella, to screen her from the scorching noonday heat; but he only laughed. "The sun could not find out such as she," he said; "she was too thin; it was only stout people that had sunstrokes;" and so he sent her away.

Do you wonder he felt frightened now, when he saw Mrs. Judson sitting at the general's right hand, and remembered how he had treated her? He must have been sure too that she was telling the English officers all the story; for though he could not understand the language that was spoken, they kept looking at him very angrily; and no wonder; for Englishmen are not in the habit of treating women so.

Mrs. Judson turned to the Burman, and told him in his own language that he had nothing to fear; but, in spite of this assurance, you may suppose the dinner was not a very pleasant one to him and his companions.

The war, which was now happily ended, taught the Burmese some new lessons, and quite changed their opinions about the English and sepoys.

They were astonished at the skill displayed by the foreigners in the use of artillery and rockets and shells. They were very much surprised to see that in fighting, if one soldier was wounded, another immediately took his place; they did not know what to think of them, and compared the English to some demons they believe in, called balus, which they say feed on human flesh.

They were so surprised that they believed quite impossible things. They said that the soldiers went on fighting even after their hands were cut off, and that the surgeons came after the troops, picked up the arms and legs which were left behind, and stuck them on the wounded men again.

But what astonished them most of all was this: the English kept their word. If they promised to do a thing, they did it. They had said they would leave Rangoon, and they left. Such conduct as this the Burmese could not understand. "The English have a regard for truth," they said, "which is extraordinary. In us Burmese there is no truth."

I hope both you and I will do all we can to keep up the character of the people that love the Bible as a truth-telling people, though we may never have an opportunity of astonishing the Burmese.

CHAPTER X.

DR. JUDSON ALONE AT AMHERST.

THE war was over; Dr. Judson was free. He returned to Rangoon with his wife, to find the mission house destroyed and the Christians scattered. It was impossible to settle there at that time with any hope of success; so the missionaries removed to Amherst, on the river Salween. This place, and the country in which it is situated, had been given up to the English at the close of the war. Here they would be protected; and they hoped at last for a comfortable and happy home.

Many of the Christians and other Burmese, who could no longer remain at Rangoon, also removed to Amherst; mission work was once more commenced, and a school was opened and placed under the care of Moung Ing.

Dr. Judson was again wanted in Ava as interpreter. He went, leaving his wife in Amherst, and hoping to return to her in two or three months. She had never been well since the illnesses of which I have told you; she was worn out with suffering, and here, at Amherst, alone and among strangers, she sickened and died. The English residents in the place were very kind to her, but no mother or sister or husband was by.

This is part of the last letter she wrote to her husband:

"Moung Ing's school has commenced with ten scholars, and more are expected. Poor little Maria is still feeble. I sometimes hope she is getting better; then again she declines to her former weakness. When I ask her where papa is, she always starts up and points towards the sea. The servants behave very well; and I have no trouble about any thing, excepting you and Maria. Pray take care of yourself, particularly as it regards the intermittent fever at Ava. May God preserve and bless you, and restore you in safety to your new and old home, is the prayer of your affectionate ANN."

Dr. Judson heard of his dear wife's death while still at Ava. He reached his home in safety; but she who had made his home so very precious to him was not there. She had been called away; but it was away from sickness and grief and pain, to be for ever joyful and well in the bright and happy home Jesus had prepared for her in heaven.

A very few months after her mother's death, the angels carried away the little Maria also, and took her to Jesus.

Dr. Judson was left alone; how lonely and sad he was who can say? Many people were kind to him and sorry for him, not only among the English, but the Christian Burmese also, who loved their kind teacher.

Too ill and unhappy to preach or teach, Dr. Judson took his Bible and went away into the jungle to read and pray. The place which he had chosen was not safe; wild beasts, and particularly tigers, roamed among the thick grass and trees. He did not know that any one followed him; but a good Christian man, named Ko Dwah, went after him, knowing that Dr. Judson was thinking so much of other things that he could not remember the tigers. At night, when the teacher he so much loved returned to his bamboo house,

Ko Dwah remained behind in the jungle, and made a seat there under the trees, and drew the branches together overhead so as to form a little arbor.

Dr. Judson went to that seat day after day for more than a month, and God kept him safely all the while; but he never knew who had done this deed of love for him. But as he sat there under the broad forest-trees, and read the sweet words that tell of God's boundless love, and felt how his love was all around him, in the sky and in the air, in the trees and grass and flowers and every thing that makes the world beautiful, and how even to this lonely spot his fellow-creatures' love had followed him, he grew happier in his loneliness, and more and more willing to devote himself to God and the Burmese.

You remember how once the prophet Elijah went a day's journey into the wilderness, and sat down weary and faint and sad under a juniper-tree. God sent an angel to him to comfort and cheer him. Does it not seem to you that Ko Dwah was, like this angel, sent by God to comfort Dr. Judson in the jungle?

CHAPTER XI.

MAULMAIN, AND NEW MISSIONARIES.

WHILE Dr. Judson was in prison, other missionaries had been waiting at Calcutta until peace should be restored in Burmah, intending then to join him. They arrived in Amherst very soon after Mrs. Judson's death, and one of them, Mrs. Wade, took charge of her baby until, as I have told you, she joined her mother in heaven.

The names of these missionaries were Mr. and Mrs. Wade, and Mr. and Mrs. Boardman. There were soon so many missionaries in Burmah, that you would not remember all their names even if you heard them; and it would be quite impossible in a little book like this to give you any idea of all the work they did—the houses they built, the zayats they made in which to preach, the schools they opened in which to teach the heathen children, the journeys they undertook, and the cities, towns, and villages which they visited.

Dr. Judson, with Mr. and Mrs. Wade and Mr. and Mrs. Boardman, did not remain at Amherst, but soon went to reside at Maulmain. This city, also, you will find on the Salween river, at its mouth. It is only twenty-five miles from Amherst, and had also come into the possession of the English at the close of the war.

Maulmain must be a fine city to look at. Beautiful hills rise on all sides, and the slopes are covered with houses and pillars, with convents, kyoungs, temples, and glittering pagodas, which rise amid groves of palms, cocoanuts, bananas, tamarinds, mangoes, and citrons. On the banks of the river are large yards, to which thousands of logs of teakwood are floated every year. Here sawyers are at work shaping the wood, and elephants are constantly employed dragging the huge tree-trunks up from the river's edge. A man called a mahout sits upon the elephant's neck, and directs him how to move and shift and arrange the logs. The docile animals do their work most patiently and cleverly. I should like to pay a visit to those timber-yards—should not you? Every yard has at least two elephants.

The principal pagoda at Maulmain, called Payah Pu, stands on a wide plateau, and has four large gateways opening to it, each gateway guarded by huge stone lions with enormous glass eyes. This pagoda, too, has a large bell, around which is engraved a Burmese inscription, and underneath the Burmese is one in English. This is the English inscription:

"This bell is made by Koonalinnguh-yah, the priest, and its weight 600 viss. No one design to destroy this bell. Maulmain, March 30, 1855. He who destroyed to this bell, they must be in the great heell and unable to coming out."

You will see from the date that this inscription, so funnily expressed and badly spelt, was written many years after the missionaries first settled at Maulmain, which was in the year 1827.

In the year 1827, instead of large busy yards crowded with timber and workmen and elephants, there was, by the river side, only a row of poor little native houses. The number of houses, however, was daily growing larger, for many of the Burmese preferred the government of the English to that of their own king. Some sepoys and English officers were staying near in cantonments; and the missionaries soon erected a little bamboo-house.

This little house was about a mile from the English cantonments, and close by was a thick jungle, in which, night after night, the cries and howls of wild beasts were heard; it was unsafe, also, on account of the murderers and robbers who prowled about.

One night, Mrs. Boardman awoke, and was surprised to find the light extinguished, which had certainly been left burning when she kissed her baby and lay down by her husband's side to go to sleep. She arose to relight the lamp, but what a scene of confusion she beheld! The trunks and boxes and chests of drawers had all been opened, and their contents turned out upon the floor. Thieves had been into the room, and had carried away every thing that appeared to them valuable. How quietly they must have done their work not to disturb the sleepers! But suppose that either Mr. or Mrs. Boardman had awakened, or that the baby had cried, what then? In the muslin musquito-curtains hanging over the bed two long gashes showed where murderers had stood with knives in their hands, ready to slay if need were, while their companions rifled the room.

Yes, murderers had stood by the bedside; but had not angels too been there—angels sent by Him who never slumbers, to keep his servants from awakening? No care of their own could have saved them in that hour of danger; but "so he giveth his beloved sleep."

After this, Sir Archibald Campbell provided a guard of sepoys to protect the house; and the population increased so rapidly, that before long the missionaries' house was nearly in the centre of the town. The wild beasts were driven farther away by the presence of man, and the unruly men were more restrained by the presence of law and order.

With so many heathen settling around them, there was plenty of work to do. Mrs. Wade and Mrs. Boardman opened schools for the little Burmese girls, and Dr. Judson and Mr. Wade built zayats, one at the north and the other at the south end of the town. In these zayats the missionaries spent most of their time; and as some of the Christians from Rangoon had settled at Maulmain, and helped the missionaries, and there was no government opposition to fear, there was great reason to hope for much progress.

There was progress, and the progress has continued all through the years from that day to this. But the Burmese have not quickly learned to love Jesus, and to see how happy his religion would make them; most of them still believe in their false god, Gaudama. Some Burmese, indeed many, have been converted to God; but it was not the proud Burmese, but a people whom they despised and enslaved and ill-treated—the poor Karens—who were to receive gladly the good news that Jesus brought.

CHAPTER XII.

THE KARENS AT DONG-YAHN, AND THEIR TRADITIONS.

BURMAH is not inhabited by the Burmese only. Away beyond the fine Burmese cities, among the beautiful mountains and in jungle villages dwell tribes of people called Karens.

Long years ago they had been subdued by their Burmese neighbors, and now many of them were slaves, and all of them were oppressed and ill-treated by their conquerors. They were wild, rough, and almost savage in their appearance; their religion was different from that of the Burmese; they spoke a different language and wore a different dress.

The missionaries had often noticed these poor people. In the autumn of the year, especially, many of them would visit Rangoon and Maulmain. They came laden with articles for sale: fowls, bees'-wax, or honey; rattans, mats, silk, or vegetables; and sometimes they brought tusks of elephants or rhinoceroses.

You see the Karens cannot be idle people, if they bring such things to the cities for sale. They are compelled to be industrious, because the Burmese oblige them to pay such heavy taxes; and it is principally to procure money to pay the taxes that they sell these goods. Their own food is generally rice or fish, and animals which they catch by hunting and angling. Their rice-fields are their great care, and these have many enemies. Wild hogs root up the young plants; peococks devour the ears before they are ripe, and immense flocks of parrots often attack the grain which has escaped the hogs and peacocks. Indeed, while the rice is growing some one has to watch the field day and night.

It was in October, when the rice was reaped and threshed, that the Karens visited the Burmese cities, to sell and buy. They often walked along the roads in parties, singing sad, wild songs, and the missionaries would catch the sounds as they passed. I think, if they could have understood what these poor people were singing, they would sooner have made their acquaintance; but years passed on, and still the Karens sang their songs, and went to and fro, and the missionaries knew not what they sang. Would you like to know?

> The Karen was the elder brother,
> And obtained all the words of God.
> God formerly loved the Karen nation above all others,
> But because of their transgression, he cursed them,
> And now they have no books.
> He will again have mercy on them,
> And love them above all others.
>
> God departed with our younger brother,
> The white foreigner.
> He conducted God away to the west.
> God gave them power to cross waters and reach lands,
> And to have rulers from among themselves.
> Then God went up to heaven.
> But he made the white foreigners
> More skilful than all other natio s.
>
> When God had departed,
> The Karens became slaves to the Burmans,
> Became sons of the forest, and children of poverty;
> Were scattered everywhere.
> The Burmans made them labor bitterly,
> Till many dropped down dead in the jungle,
> Or they twisted their arms behind them,
> Beat them with stripes,

And pounded them with the elbow,
Days without end.

In the midst of their suffering;
They remembered the ancient sayings of the elders,
That God would yet save them,
That a Karen king would yet appear.
The Talien kings have had their season,
The Burman kings have had their season ;
The Siamese kings have had their season ;
And the foreign kings will have their season ;
But the Karen king will yet appear.
When he arrives, there will be but one monarch,
And there will be neither rich nor poor.
Every thing will be happy,
And even lions and leopards will lose their savageness.

Hence, in their deep affliction they prayed :
If God will save us,
Let him save speedily!
We can endure these sufferings no longer,
Alas, where is God?
Our ancestors said that when our younger brothers came back.
The white foreigners,
Who were able to keep company with God,
The Karens will be happy.

Our ancestors charged us thus :
Children and grandchildren,
If the king come by land, weep ;
If by water, laugh.
It will not come in our days,
But it will in yours.
Hence the Karens longed for those
Who were to come by water.

It was such words as these the Karens sung. And the white foreigners had come by water. There they were sitting in their zayats, with the books in their hands which the Karens were waiting for. They were translating it for the Karens' conquerors, and were telling them the good news of the King of peace, who was to reign over all the earth.

But the good news was on its way to the Karens also. At Maulmain, one of these despised people came to live with Dr. Judson. This is how it happened.

Some of the Burmese converts at Rangoon knew that their teachers had wished for opportunities to instruct the Karens; and one of them, Koshwaba, paid a debt for a poor Karen slave, Kothahbyn, and so set him free. Koshwaba then took him into his house to live, intending to try and teach him the new religion. But Kothahbyn proved a very troublesome inmate. He was so rude and so passionate that Koshwaba could not keep him, and thought it was of very little use to try and do him good, for all his efforts appeared to be thrown away.

This was at the time that Dr. Judson and

Mr. and Mrs. Wade had gone to Maulmain and were living there together; and they resolved that, rather than give up hope about this troublesome Karen, they would take him into their house. But what a change came over Kothahbyn! He began to pray; he became sorry for his sins; and with tears he confessed them, and asked God to forgive him, for Christ's sake. He gave all his heart to the Saviour who had died for him; and from that time, for thirteen years, he went about among his countrymen, telling them the glad news that the white foreigners had brought. The poor Karens had the gospel preached to them, and very many of them had to thank God that they saw and heard Kothahbyn.

Soon after Kothahbyn came to live with them, Dr. Judson and Mr. Wade made some journeys to the Karen villages. They procured a boat, and, accompanied by a few Burmese Christians, they went up the river Salween, and visited some villages in a district called Dong-yahn, which was about thirty miles from Maulmain.

No sooner did the villagers catch sight of

their strange visitors, than they all ran away and hid themselves in the jungle. The missionaries, however, went straight up to the deserted huts, and sat down in the shade of the trees. Of course the Karens were watching from their hiding-places, and by-and-by one or two ventured out, and came nearer and nearer, until they were quite close to the strangers.

"Why have you come to our village?" asked the Karens.

"We have come," replied the missionaries, "to tell you about the true God and the way of salvation."

"Is it so? We feared you had been sent by the government to make us slaves, and we were afraid. But if you are teachers of religion, come to tell us of God, we are happy, and will listen."

Soon a large group of listeners were crowding around the white foreigners. The people were no longer afraid, when they discovered the object of their visitors, but were very pleased and joyful. They examined the missionaries' dress, and wondered at the whiteness of their faces; but most of all they were interested to hear about God. As the missionaries did not know the Karen language, one of the Burmese, who understood it, interpreted for them.

"Have you brought us God's book?" asked the Karens.

"Yes, we have brought you God's book; but what do you know about God's book? Have you any books?"

"No, we have no books now; but our fathers say that long ago we had God's book written on leather, and in it we were told never to worship idols. The prophet who had charge of the book was one day reading it under a tree. He fell asleep with the book on his knees, and while he slept a dog came and tore it up. Then God was angry because his book had not been taken care of. Now we have no books; but white foreigners will come and bring us God's book once again. This our prophets say."

"See, the white foreigners have come!" they cried. "You have brought God's book."

"Yes, here is God's book!" and the missionaries showed to the eager people an English Bible; "but it is in the language of the foreigners; you cannot understand it. We have translated part of it into Burmese. Can you read Burmese?"

"No," they answered, "we cannot; but we will learn, and you will write it in our language for us."

Dr. Judson said he would ask that a teacher might be sent from the land of the white foreigners, who would learn their language, and write books for them.

"And how long will it be," they asked, "before the teacher can come, and learn the language, and give us God's book, so that we may read it?"

"Ten years," answered Dr. Judson.

"Ten years! then it will not be in my time," sighed one old man.

"You must not wait for a new teacher; you must begin at once to tell us what God says in his book."

And they did begin at once. For two weeks the missionaries remained in the village; they were entertained in the chief's house, and spent their time talking with all those who came to them. As the glad news of the white foreigners who had come with God's book spread from one to another, Karens came down from the hills around, hurrying over streams and mountain passes, from their desert and jungle homes, to see and hear for themselves.

It appears as though the Karens must somewhere have really known the Bible; they seem to have derived so many of their traditions from it, and sometimes even use Bible words. Do you think that people who had not heard the account of Adam and Eve in the garden of Eden could have composed this song?

> Anciently, God commanded;
> But Satan appeared, bringing destruction.
> Formerly, God commanded;
> But Satan appeared, deceiving unto death.
> The woman Eu and the man Tha-nai
> Pleased not the eye of the dragon.
> The dragon looked on them—
> The dragon beguiled the woman and Tha-nai.
> How is this said to have happened?
> The great dragon succeeded in deceiving—
> Deceiving unto death.
> How do they say it was done?
> A yellow fruit the great dragon took,
> And gave to the children of God.
> A white fruit took the great dragon,
> And gave to the daughter and son of God.
> They transgressed the commands of God,
> And God turned away from them.

They kept not all the words of God—
  Were deceived ; deceived unto sickness.
They kept not all the law of God—
  Were deceived ; deceived unto death.

The Karens believe that Satan was once a holy being, but for some sin he was cast out of heaven, and then he deceived the son and daughter of God. Satan came into the garden and said to them :

"Why are you here?"

"Our Father, God, put us here."

"What do you eat?"

"The fruit of many trees ; but of one tree God said : 'Eat not; if you eat, you will die.'"

Then said Satan : "The heart of your Father God is not with you ; this is the sweetest of all. Let each one eat a single fruit, then you will know."

The man replied : "Our Father God said : 'Eat not ;'" and so saying, he went away ; but the woman listened to Satan, who said to her : "Now go give the fruit to your husband." So she coaxed her husband, and Satan laughed.

On the following morning they were silent

before God; and God said: "You have ate the fruit that is not good; you shall die."

How glad the Karens must have been when they really found that this story was written in God's book! and not only this story of the way in which man sinned, and God said, "Ye shall die," but also that glorious story of which they knew nothing—the story of Jesus, who came to save sinners, and said: "I am come that ye might have life."

When the missionaries returned to Maulmain, Mr. Wade set to work at once to learn the Karen language, and to write it. This was difficult, as they had no books; but it was not long before he could speak a little; and as some of the young Karens came to the mission station to learn Burmese, long before ten years were over they had books and parts of the Bible written in their language, and many of them had lost their wildness and savageness, and were striving to grow like the meek and gentle Jesus.

CHAPTER XIII.

A Priest's Funeral—The Story of Guapung.

STILL some years passed before a missionary was sent to live at Dong-yahn. The first who went was a young lady, Miss Eleanor Macomber. When she arrived, she found the village almost empty; the people were away attending the burning of a priest, and almost all returned tipsy.

The burning of a priest is quite a holiday and festival. Great preparations are made for the ceremony. The poor dead body is covered with gold leaf, and drawn in procession through the town, lying in a richly-ornamented coffin. When the procession approaches the enclosure in which the burning is to take place, the men will pretend to go different ways, and drag and tug and pull.

Quite a large space is generally chosen, for sometimes as many as twelve thousand people gather together to see the sight. They all come dressed in their best, decked out with silks and gauzes, lace, golden ornaments, and earrings.

The women bring offerings of fruits and flowers, one after the other, until you might count seventy or eighty baskets full perhaps. Then a few prayers are said; and when these are concluded the fun begins.

The gayly-dressed people, with their thousands of paper umbrellas, swarm over the ground, and many of them erect tiny sheds with bright handkerchiefs or broad leaves supported on bamboos, to shelter them from the heat of the sun. It is a gay scene. But there in the centre is the funeral-pile, and on it the coffin, stripped now of its richest ornaments.

Presently there comes tearing across the ground a little carriage. No one guides it; no one can stop it. You might see by the cloud of smoke, and hear by the loud hissing noise it makes, that it is full of gunpowder, and that this little carriage is really a kind of rocket. The people run from before it as it approaches. It is intended to reach the fu-

THE BURIAL OF A PRIEST.

neral-pile and set it on fire; but a little rising in the ground turns it over and stops it before it is nearly there; and then the people shout and dance and sing, and prepare to send another.

Every village in the district provides one of these rocket carriages, and each tries to make its own the smartest and best. All have some strange device upon them—an animal, not much like any that really roam the fields or forests, or an archer perhaps, or a crab. Many of these unguided rockets, of course, miss their destination, and sometimes they accidentally turn quite round, and run among the people, doing a great deal of mischief. If at length one succeeds, and the funeral-pile is really set on fire, there is great rejoicing, and the people of the village to which the fortunate rocket belongs expect to have good fortune all the year. It oftener happens, however, that all the rocket carriages fail, and the priests themselves set fire to the pile. The day ends with drinking and revelling, and many sad sounds and sights of wickedness and quarrelling.

How different such a scene from that which we witness in our quiet churchyards and cemeteries, when Christians who have fallen asleep in Jesus are laid by their friends in their graves till the morning when Jesus, who is the Resurrection and the Life, shall call them forth. What gentle words of hope and comfort are uttered there—words that quiet and soothe, and help to make us patient and good, so that those who hear them go home to pray that they may be ready to meet again the friend that God has taken from them.

The people of Dong-yahn came home after the burning of this priest in a very different frame of mind; but the teacher who was to teach them to love better things had arrived. I think she was a very brave woman to stop there alone among such wild, bad people; but nothing makes us so truly brave as love to Jesus. Miss Macomber did not give up hope, but remained, and lived in the house of the chief.

I must tell you the story of one poor woman who lived in the Dong-yahn district.

This woman's name was Guapung. She was the wife of a chief; but because she was a woman, she had always been treated as a slave, and had been compelled to carry burdens and to walk behind her husband and brother. Her husband, too, was often angry with her, and beat her if she did not do just as he wished.

One time, when Dr. Judson had gone up the Salween to visit the Karen villages, Guapung had watched his boat as it approached, and had ventured to the river bank to see the strangers land. Dr. Judson noticed her, and holding out his hand kindly, asked her how she was. The poor woman was astonished; she was not accustomed to be treated so well. She said to her brother afterwards: "I have seen one of the sons of God."

"Did he speak?"

"Yes, and he gave me his hand."

Guapung's brother thought she had not behaved rightly in shaking hands with a foreigner, and he repeated what she had said to her husband. Her husband was so angry when he heard it that he beat her severely.

Guapung considered in her heart how differently the white man and her husband had behaved, and she said to herself: "Ever since I was a child I have served Gaudama, but he has never kept my husband from beating me; this white man spoke kindly to me; his God must be the true God. I will worship him."

So she made a prayer to the foreigner's God, whom she did not know, and this was the prayer she made:

"Great King! Mighty Judge, Father God, Lord God, Uncle or Honorable God, the Righteous One! In the heavens, in the earth, in the mountains, in the seas, in the north, in the south, in the east, in the west, pity me, I pray! Show me thy glory, that I may know thee, who thou art."

For five years Guapung prayed that prayer constantly, and then another white teacher came to the village. I cannot tell you who he was, but Guapung went and sat at his feet to listen to his words, as Mary sat at the feet of Jesus. This teacher stayed for nine days, and then left. At last Eleanor Macomber came, and Guapung by degrees learned who the God and the Righteous One was to whom she had so long prayed. She came to love the God whom we worship with all her heart, for she learned how wonderfully he had loved her. She was a great help to Miss Macomber during the time she resided at Dong-yahn, and also to the missionaries who succeeded her—Mr. and Mrs. Bullard.

Guapung tried very much to teach the people at Dong-yahn to love one another; she did all she could to show the women how they might persuade their husbands to be kinder, and that it was possible to make their children obedient without beating them.

I do not think you would like to have been the child of one of these Karen women. Mrs. Bullard says she once saw a mother beat her little naked girl till she was quite covered with cuts and wales; and another grew so tired of nursing her sick baby that she flung it down on the floor. The poor baby died the next day. You were never treated in such a manner by your mother, I know; she takes you kindly and lovingly into her arms, as Jesus would have done had you lived wher he was on earth.

The missionaries and Guapung went among the women constantly, and tried to teach them better. "If you want your husbands and children to love you," they said, "you must be kind to them, as Jesus has been kind to us; you must not get cross and scold, but be gentle and patient, and make their homes comfortable for them."

Many of the women really did try; and one succeeded so well that her husband was made quite glad and happy. Another man, who had not a good wife, when he saw this change, came over from his village to visit "Guapung, the big teacheress who had the charm." He told her he had heard that Christ's religion did not allow wives to scold their husbands; and the men in his village all wished their wives to become Christians, for they did not like to be scolded. I dare say Guapung told him that the religion of Christ did not allow men to ill-treat their wives, and that, if they wanted happy homes, the men as well as the women would do well to become Christians.

No doubt there are still many bad people in the Dong-yahn villages, for the good and bad are living together everywhere now; but there is a great change for the better since Miss Macomber went and found all the people away at the burning of the priest. The "white book," as the Karens call the Bible, has made all the difference there: now there are schools in which the children learn to read it; classes in which the men and women study it; chapels in which from Sunday to Sunday they hear it explained; and not only in the schools and chapels are they worshipping God, but in heaven many grown people and little children from these Karen villages are singing with the angels around his throne.

CHAPTER XIV.

MR. AND MRS. BOARDMAN GO TO TAVOY—THE REBELLION.

WHEN the missionaries found how eager the Karens were to have God's word, they thought it would be right and pleasant to go to other parts of the country and spread the good news among them.

Mr. and Mrs. Boardman left Maulmain and went to Tavoy, a place which you will find marked near the seacoast lower down on the map.

Tavoy is a large, straggling town, inhabited by Burmese, but governed by the English, for it was taken by them at the same time that they took possession of Maulmain. Near Tavoy there is a remarkable loadstone rock, and at the mouth of the river on which the town is built there are some red rocks, called "the cows." This is the foolish story the Burmese tell about them:

Once upon a time a drove of cows was swimming across the river, intending to destroy a pagoda which stood on the opposite side. The idol, however, was fortunately looking out from the pagoda towards the river, and when he saw the cows coming, he exclaimed: "These are not cows, but rocks." Immediately the whole drove stopped, and there they have stopped ever since, for they turned into stones in the middle of the river.

Tavoy is thirty-four miles from the mouth of the river. The scenery around is very pretty, and many of the houses are quite concealed by beautiful flowering shrubs, or fine tropical trees, such as palms, plantains, jacks, and cassias.

One little temple at Tavoy is very curious; it is called the Peepul Fane, for the branches of an old peepul-tree have taken root close about the idol, and have made quite a bower around it. The peepul is a very pretty tree, and rather scarce. The Buddhists consider it very sacred, because the story is that Gaudama once went to sleep under a peepul, and dreamed that he was so big he needed the whole earth for a bed, and the Himalaya mountains for a pillow.

At the time that Mr. and Mrs. Boardman went to Tavoy, there were in the city more than a thousand pagodas and two hundred heathen priests. No wonder the missionaries wished to go among the people and tell them of the one true priest Jesus Christ.

Kothahbyn, the Karen convert of whom you have heard, went to Tavoy with Mr. and Mrs. Boardman. He used to go out into the mountain and jungle villages, and tell his countrymen that the white foreigners had at last come with God's book. The Karens here were quite as delighted as those at Dong-yahn; they flocked to Tavoy to see the white teacher, and to listen to what God's book said.

Mr. Boardman also went out into the Karen villages. At one village he found there was a book kept very carefully and reverently by the chief of the tribe. The people could not read a word of it, but they believed that some day a teacher would come to explain the book to them; and now they asked Mr. Boardman to look at it, and tell them what it meant. It was brought to him in a basket, where it lay very carefully wrapped up in muslin. With great reverence the parcel was unrolled, until there was exposed to view an old, worn-out English book. What book do you think it was? A copy of the Book of Common Prayer. It had certainly been in England once, for it had been printed at Oxford; but little the printers, or binders, or the bookseller, or even the purchaser had thought that, by-and-by, the book would be so much regarded by a tribe of heathen people.

"It is a good book," said Mr. Boardman; "it teaches that there is a God in heaven. But you make a mistake in worshipping the book; you must worship the God of whom the book speaks;" and he read them some verses from the psalms about God. How delighted the poor people must have been to find a meaning to their treasure!

The old man who had kept this precious book afterwards became a Christian, and so also did many people of his tribe.

Mr. Boardman built a bamboo house outside one of the city gates, and here he and his wife resided. Some Burmese boys came to live with them, so that they had quite a boarding-school; and besides, Mrs. Boardman taught some girls in a day-school at a little distance. A great many descriptions of the schools were of course sent to her friends in America; and she appears to have been very industrious, and to have begun her work very early in the morning. In one of her letters she says: "I am just returned from one of the day-schools. The sun had not risen when I arrived, but the little girls were in the house ready for instruction. My walk to this school is through a retired road, shaded on one side by the old wall of the city, which is overgrown by wild creepers and pole flowers, and on the other by large fruit trees."

While Mrs. Boardman attended to the girls' schools, Mr. Boardman was busy with the boys, and with the native Christians and inquirers who frequented the mission house. Mrs. Boardman in her letters home told of her husband's work also. "In the room before me sits my dear husband," she writes, "surrounded by nine little heathen boys, to whom he is imparting a knowledge of that gospel which can save from eternal ruin. On each side of the house is a long verandah. In one of these the native Christians are holding a prayer-meeting in Burmese, and in the other sits the Chinese convert Kee-Zea-Chung, loudly urging three or four of his deluded countrymen to turn from the worship of idols to that of the true God."

Besides the schools to keep Mr. and Mrs. Boardman busy, there was little Sarah, the baby, who slept so quietly when the house at Maulmain was robbed; she must have wanted a good share of time and attention bestowed upon her; and soon another baby came, a little son, whom they named George. Little Sarah, however, shortly died, and was laid to rest in a beautiful grove of trees not far from the house. Her papa and mamma were full of grief at her loss, and missed her merry face and winning ways sadly; but afterwards they knew that God had taken her away from the evil to come.

One night, when all in the mission house were peacefully sleeping, there was a noise outside of men walking and talking. One of the Burmese boys was awakened by the sound. He got up and peeped out through the crevices left in the slight bamboo wall of his sleeping room. He saw a party of men passing by, in the direction of the city. They were talking of buffaloes which had strayed away. Other men followed; all were talking about buffaloes, and all were going towards the city. As far as the boy could see there were dusky forms of men among the trees. He grew quite frightened. What were the men about? It could not really be buffaloes which they wanted. No; it was a rebellion against the English government, and the men wanted, not buffaloes, but the powder stores in the city, and the lives of the English there.

Suddenly there was a fierce yell, and then guns were fired. Mr. and Mrs. Boardman awoke in great fright; but they could do nothing. A party of two hundred rebels armed with clubs, knives, spears, and guns, had attacked the powder magazine. The governor, Mr. Burney, was absent from the town; and, as no one expected the insurrection, there were only six sepoys on duty at the stores. The powder stores were very near the gate outside which the mission house was built; and not only were the firing and shouting plainly heard, but the shots flew so close that

Mrs. Boardman took her baby and crouched down in a wooden shed behind the house for safety.

By-and-by, to the great relief of the missionaries, the firing ceased—the powder stores were safe still, and in spite of their superior numbers, the rebels had been driven back.

It was day now, and as soon as the roads were safe Mr. and Mrs. Boardman left their house and made their way into the town. They were received very kindly by the governor's wife; but she was in such great difficulty herself that she could do but little to help others. It was evident that the rebels would soon return to the attack in greater force than before, and how could the few foreigners and sepoys defend themselves against their enemies?

On the wharf was a wooden house built on piles overhanging the river, and an enclosure in which they might take refuge. The sepoys hastened to convey there a quantity of gunpowder and three cannon—the rest of the gunpowder was thrown down wells in the town, that it might not fall into the enemies' hands.

Amid sad scenes of fighting and bloodshed, along streets in which wounded men lay dying and groaning, the little party of Europeans and soldiers made their way from the government house to the house on the wharf. Mrs. Burney and Mrs. Boardman, the only ladies among them, each carried an infant; and a strange mixed group it must have been that went with them. The few Europeans, not a dozen altogether, with their dark servants, and their defenders the sepoys, accompanied by their wives and children. There were in all three or four hundred persons, besides their arms, baggage, and provisions, huddled together under one roof. But how long would they be there? How could they obtain help? There was no boat they could send down the river safely, to carry tidings of their distress; and even if tidings were sent, would it be possible for help to reach them in time, before the rebels had overcome and murdered them?

In the afternoon the rebels made a new attack. Now they had mounted cannon. A ball came whizzing through the air in the direction of the wharf enclosure. But it fell wide of the mark, and time after time as they tried to take aim they failed—no ball touched the house. The sun was sinking rapidly; in the darkness of night the firing must cease. But what of to-morrow? To-morrow had not dawned yet; but even the night did not bring peace.

In the quiet darkness a little boat came gliding stealthily along the water, and glided silently under the overhanging walls of the crowded house. Why was the boat there? As it lay quietly in the darkness, a little spark of light might have been seen—a little sparkle which meant death to all those men, women, and children.

Happily a sepoy lying on the floor saw the light beneath him through a crevice, and in a moment he understood what it meant. He raised himself on his elbow, seized his gun, aimed through the crevice, and fired. There was a shriek in the house from the startled sleepers, a heavy splash in the water below; the little spark was gone, and presently an empty boat floated away on the river. The sepoy who had fired that shot had saved them all from being burnt to death; and the man who had carried the match, and had intended to set fire to the building, was lying dead in the water.

In the morning the firing from the cannon recommenced. Happily, the rebels could not aim well, and happily too their gunpowder was very bad. That which they had tried to obtain was lying out of reach in the wells, or was in the enclosure with the English, being used to shoot them. It was in vain their trying—they could not strike the house. Not only that day, but all the next, and the next, they tried, and still they could not succeed. In the meantime the besieged party watched in fear and trembling each new attempt, and prayed fervently for the help which only God could send them.

The fifth evening came from the time the revolt had commenced. The night was lit by the blaze of burning houses. The rebels had set the town on fire; and now, with a terrible war-cry, they rushed from the open spaces between the burning houses, five hundred strong, upon the wharf enclosure. The sepoys met them as they came with a sharp fire, which killed and wounded many of them; and just then there fell so heavy a shower of rain, that the flames which had lighted them were extinguished, and they were forced to flee in the darkness, carrying with them as they could their wounded companions. Was not that shower-help sent from God?

The next day the firing began again, and things looked worse and worse. The provisions were nearly consumed, the soldiers were worn out and dispirited by the heat and want of rest, and many of the foreigners were quite ill. The sun rose again over the ruined town and this little besieged party. But with the sun came relief.

Far down the river, quite out on the horizon, there was an appearance of smoke. Mrs. Burney was called to see it. She looked at it, and looked again. It was getting a little plainer, even while she gazed. Surely it was a steamer coming up the river, and if so, no doubt her husband the governor was on board.

Can you imagine the joy of all those poor people as they watched the steamer through the windings of the river—the deliverance which God had sent them just at the time it was most needed—for all those days they had not been able to send word to any one of their danger?

Colonel Burney was very much surprised when he saw the enclosure crowded with soldiers and foreigners, the mounted cannon, and the ruins of the town. He had had no idea, as he came up the river, of the terrible state in which he was to find his home. But now that he was come, there was a leader for the soldiers, and ill and dispirited as they were, they felt that they could fight again.

Mrs. Burney and her baby, and Mrs. Boardman with her little Georgie, were sent on board the steamer at once; and there, in spite of the shots which the rebels fired after them, they felt safe, and rested comfortably in the cabin as the vessel puffed away with them down the river on its way to Maulmain.

The next day the steamer was again started to Tavoy, this time laden with European soldiers; but when they arrived at the wharf, the rebellion was already suppressed, and those who had been foremost in the revolt were safely lodged in prison.

CHAPTER XV.

MR. BOARDMAN'S WORK FINISHED—DR. MASON TAKES HIS PLACE AT TAVOY.

WHEN Mr. Boardman rejoined his wife, she was startled to see how very thin and ill he looked. This terrible time of the rebellion had worn him very much, but even before that he had not been well; he had worked so very hard at Tavoy in preaching Christ's gospel, that he had often walked twenty miles in one day, preaching and teaching as he went; and then at night had lain down in some open zayat, where he had gone to sleep without a bed, just lying on a straw mat, and without any supper except perhaps a little rice. He did this that he might tell as many Karens as possible of God's book, and teach them the way of life. He valued Karen souls more than his own body; and in doing this he had acted as Jesus did, who laid down his life for us.

For a few months Mr. and Mrs. Boardman remained at Maulmain; but although he was feeling very ill, Mr. Boardman wished to return to his work at Tavoy. The Karens welcomed him back with much joy, though they were grieved to find how weak their kind teacher was.

A fortnight after his return, a large party of Karens from the jungle came to visit him, and stayed for several days. Sometimes Mr. Boardman could sit up in a chair and speak to them for a few minutes; but oftener he was obliged to lie still on his bed and whisper to his wife what he wished her to say to them.

Many of this party of Karens were Christians, and asked to be baptized. They carried Mr. Boardman out on his bed to a beautiful pond; here all knelt down on the grass and prayed for God's blessing, and then Moung Ing baptized nineteen.

It must have been a great comfort to Mr. Boardman that Moung Ing should be with him just now. He had been sent to Mergui by the missionaries at Maulmain, and happened to arrive at Tavoy in time to assist the missionary in this season of weakness. I say "happened," but I believe it is the good God who arranges these things; and no doubt Mr. Boardman believed it also, and thanked his Father in heaven for sending to him Moung Ing.

A new missionary, Mr. Mason, was also on his way to Tavoy. Mr. Boardman went on to the jetty to meet him; but as he was quite unable to walk, he was carried down by some of the native Christians in a chair. He was getting constantly weaker and weaker, and very soon he knew he should die. But though he was now so very ill, he did not on that account stop working for Christ.

He had promised, should his life be spared long enough, to make a journey into the jungle and visit a number of Karen villages, in order to baptize some of the people who had become Christians. Eight days after Mr. Mason reached Tavoy, Mr. Boardman started on this journey; Mr. Mason, Mrs. Boardman, and little Georgie went also, and the dying missionary was carried in his bed by a party of Karen Christians.

In order to save him the fatigue of visiting all the villages in which the Christians were living, the Karens had fixed upon one spot at which all who wished to be baptized, or to see their beloved friend again, might assemble. It was a lovely valley, through which flowed a stream of water, and all around arose beautiful mountains. Here the Karens had erected a bamboo zayat and two little rooms, one for Mr. Mason, and the other for Mr. and Mrs. Boardman and Georgie.

The Karens, although they had learned much, had very little idea of what we should call comfort. They had made Mr. Boardman's room so low, that it was not possible to stand upright in it; and as it was not larger than the compartment of a railway carriage, it must have been a difficult room in which to nurse any one so ill as Mr. Boardman. To him, however, the room was of very small concern; he was full of thoughts for those he was about to leave, and of the home to which he was going.

A hundred people had assembled from the villages around, half of whom wished to be baptized. They camped out on the open ground, under the beautiful forest trees, round about the zayat they had built. The missionaries examined those who said they were Christians, in order to see that they really understood and believed what they professed, and then they baptized thirty-four. It made Mr. Boardman very happy to think that so many of the Karens had learned to love the Saviour, and wished to devote themselves to his service.

In the evening of the day on which they had been baptized, all the Christians gathered around Mr. Boardman, who had been carried into the zayat, and he spoke to them for the last time. He said: "I did hope to stay with you till after the Lord's day, but God is calling me away. When I am gone, remember what I have taught you; that when you die, we may meet one another in the presence of God, never more to part. The teacheress will be very much distressed. Strive to lighten her burdens, and comfort her by your good conduct. Listen to the word of the new teacher and teacheress as you have done to mine. Do not neglect prayer. The eternal God to whom you pray is unchangeable. Earthly teachers sicken and die, but God remains for ever the same. Love Jesus Christ with all your hearts, and you will be for ever safe." He then offered a short prayer for them, and with Mr. Mason's help distributed to them tracts and portions of Scripture.

The next morning Mr. and Mrs. Boardman started on their way home. Mr. Boardman was, as before, carried in his bed, and many of the Karens followed. It was a sad procession, as it wound along among the forest trees and over the rough mountain-paths. The only happy one in the party was the one for whom all the rest were grieving—the teacher who was carried so sick upon his bed.

At four o'clock in the afternoon a violent storm of thunder and lightning and rain came on, much more violent than we are accustomed to see in America. There was no shelter anywhere, and no house in sight. They covered Mr. Boardman with mats and blankets, and held umbrellas over him, but the rain beat so heavily, that, in spite of all, his mattress and pillows were quite wet. This discomfort did not trouble Mr. Boardman, but it must have made his poor wife and the affectionate Karens very unhappy on his account. He was so near home that he did not feel it much. If you go to a boarding-school you will understand this. Just when the holidays are about to begin, if any thing happens to vex you, you say: "Never mind; to-morrow I shall be at home." So it was with this dying missionary; to-morrow he was going home to his Father in heaven, and the thought of the joy that was so soon to be his prevented any present discomfort from vexing him.

Before long they approached a Burmese house; but though, with tears in her eyes, Mrs. Boardman begged shelter for her husband, the inhabitants refused to let them come inside, and only after a great deal of persuasion gave them permission to spend the night in the verandah. The Burmese were so inhospitable because they knew Mr. Boardman was a teacher of a foreign religion, and that the Karens accompanying him had become Christians.

It still went on raining, and Mr. Boardman was obliged to lie on the bamboo floor, his mattress was so wet. There were such large holes in the floor, too, that Mrs. Boardman had to look carefully for a place where little Georgie might sleep without falling through. Little Georgie slept, dreaming nothing of his mother's grief. Before the darkness closed in, Mr. Mason had read the psalm in which are the words: "The angel of the Lord encampeth round about them that fear him, and delivereth them. Oh taste and see that the Lord is good: blessed is the man that trusteth in him. The righteous cry, and the Lord heareth, and delivereth them out of all their troubles." Can you not believe that angels were indeed round about that verandah, comforting that sad wife and mother? In the silent night she and her husband talked together of God's goodness; of the goodness that had not only blessed them while they were together, but that would continue to bless her and her little boy when they were left. "Leave the fatherless children, I will preserve them alive; and let thy widows trust in me." Mr. Boardman remembered that God had said this, and he knew he might trust God, and that though they were left in a far-off foreign land, his dear wife and child were safe.

In the morning Mrs. Boardman asked the Burmese for a fowl, in order to make a little broth for her husband; but though she could see three or four pecking about under the house, they told her they had none, and would give her nothing.

That day the journey was continued by the river. Mr. Boardman was once more carried to the boat by the Karens; but here the angels came and took him home, and when the boat stopped, three miles from the mission house, it was not the dearly-loved teacher that the weeping men lifted on shore and conveyed so carefully and tenderly and slowly towards the town. Moung Ing saw them approach, and went to meet them. He burst into tears as he came near; and when they reached the house, there was great weeping among the native Christians, both Karens and Burmese, who had assembled there.

The next day Mr. Boardman's remains were buried in the grove of trees where his little Sarah's body lay, and all the Europeans, and many of the natives in Tavoy, attended the furneral to show their respect and grief. Mr. Boardman had only been three years at Tavoy altogether, but many had in that time left their idol-gods and false religion, and had become Christians; so earnestly had he worked, and so much had God blessed his labors.

Mrs. Boardman was very sad, and though she had her little Georgie, she was very lonely. Still she resolved to remain at Tavoy with Mr. and Mrs. Mason, and continue teaching in the schools she had opened. She stayed at Tavoy for several years, working constantly; and God comforted her in her loneliness, and Georgie grew into a bright little boy, and was a comfort to her also.

Often during these years Mrs. Boardman went out into the Karen jungles to instruct the villagers, as her husband had done when he was on earth. Some of the kind Christian Karens would accompany her, as it would have been impossible for her to have gone alone. Indeed, it was very brave of her to go at all, for travelling in Burmah is very different from travelling in England. There were rivers to cross, but no bridges over them; there were forests to traverse, but hardly a path through them; tigers and elephants roamed in the forests, and crocodiles basked in the river mud. For men with guns, who enjoy hunting and exploring, such travelling may be pleasant; but I think very few ladies would attempt it with no other escort than a party of half-savage men.

When Mrs. Boardman took these journeys, Georgie used to accompany her, mounted on the shoulders of one of the men; and many strange animals and plants that we only read of in books, and many sights and sounds that we can only imagine, the little fellow must have learned to know in that wild country.

CHAPTER XVI.

DR. JUDSON AT RANGOON AGAIN—HE BRINGS MRS. BOARDMAN TO MAULMAIN.

DURING the years that Mr. Boardman had been at Tavoy, Dr. Judson had found plenty to do at Maulmain. He did not, on account of his sorrow, neglect the work God had given him to do. For some time he had made his home in the same house with Mr. and Mrs. Wade; but the Wades left on a visit to their friends in America, for the recovery of their health, which had suffered from the climate; and though by-and-by they returned to Maulmain, Dr. Judson was obliged for the present to make a home elsewhere.

Writing in a letter to his mother in America, he says: "After the Wades left I boarded with the Bennetts. After the Bennetts left for Rangoon I boarded with the Cutters. After the Cutters left for Ava I boarded with the Hancocks, where I now am. I have no family or living creature about me that I can call my own, except one dog, Fidelia, which belonged to Maria, and which I valued more on that account. Since the death of her little mistress she has ever been with me, but she is now growing old and will die before long; and I am sure I shall shed more than one tear when poor Fidee goes."

From this letter you see that not only had more missionaries come out to Maulmain, but also that they did not forget Ava and Rangoon. It was almost in vain, however, for missionaries to go to these cities; they were soon compelled to leave again by the persecutions of the king and governors. Dr. Judson himself went back to Rangoon two or three times, but he was not able to remain.

Once he visited Rangoon when there was a great festival held in honor of Gaudama at the Shway Dagon pagoda, the pagoda in which, you will remember, a few of the god's hairs were said to be preserved. This festival was held every year, and the people flocked into Rangoon from all parts of the country, and from as far off even as China, in order to be present.

Very many of the people had heard of the teachers of the new religion; and when it was known that Dr. Judson was in the town, numbers came to the house in which he was staying to beg for a book.

"Are you Jesus Christ's man?" they would say. "Give us a writing that tells about Jesus Christ." Or: "Sir, we have seen a writing that tells about an eternal God. Are you the man that gives away such writings? If so, pray give us one, for we want to know the truth before we die."

Some of the tracts had pictures on them, and if a man was fortunate enough to receive one of these, he could hardly keep from screaming and jumping for joy. Pretty pictures were not common there as they are in our happy country.

No tracts were given away unless they were asked for. Dr. Judson did not offer them to any one; but you will, I am sure, be surprised at the numbers that were wanted. "On Tuesday," says Dr. Judson, "we gave away three hundred; on Wednesday, eight hundred; on

Thursday, nine hundred; on Friday, seven hundred; on Saturday, eleven hundred; on Sunday, eight hundred; on Monday, five hundred." The next day the boats which had crowded the river began to disperse; the people were returning home; but Moung Sanlone, one of the native Christians who was with Dr. Judson, begged to have two thousand given to him, with which to go up the river and supply the boats as they left. He could not have them, simply because there were not enough left. Although the crowds were dispersing, as many tracts seemed wanted as ever; and Dr. Judson would look at his diminishing stores, and take out two hundred, and try in vain to make them last through the day. He sent constantly to Maulmain for more, and the gentlemen there worked day and night at the press, and yet could not print them fast enough. There were in all ten thousand tracts given away at that festival. This was just at the time that Mr. Boardman died at Tavoy.

Dr. Judson during these years did not neglect the Karens. There were much greater numbers of these people around Maulmain and Rangoon than at Tavoy. Many of them now were being instructed in the mission schools, and Mr. Wade at Maulmain and Mr. Mason at Tavoy were busy learning their language and translating the Bible for them. Journeys were constantly taken with the view of visiting their villages, and Kothahbyn was spending his life in proclaiming the good news among them.

But the great work upon which Dr. Judson was engaged all these years was the translation of the Bible into Burmese. You remember the precious pillow which contained the parts already translated, and which had been so wonderfully preserved during his time of imprisonment. It was not until eight years after that the translation of the Bible was finished. But in the year 1834, Dr. Judson had the great happiness of seeing the whole Bible complete in Burmese; and he thanked God for having allowed him to translate his holy word into a language in which so many millions of heathens might read it.

The same year that the translation of the Bible was finished, Dr. Judson paid a visit to Tavoy. Here he asked Mrs. Boardman to become his wife. She consented, and they were married. She bade farewell to the home in Tavoy, where she had lived so long, to the Karens, and her school-children there, and with Georgie and her new husband embarked for Maulmain.

Moung Ing died at Mergui the year that Dr. Judson and Mrs. Boardman were married. He had been a great help to the missionaries for many years; he had been with Dr. and Mrs. Judson in Ava, and with Mr. and Mrs. Boardman at Tavoy, and at Mergui he was preaching the gospel when he became ill and died.

The next year the old Bengalee cook, Koochil, became a Christian. While Dr. Judson grieved at the loss of Moung Ing, he must have rejoiced indeed to see this change in Koochil. Ever since the time of the imprisonment at Ava, he had been employed by some one of the mission families. Now he was an old man, over sixty years of age, with sunken cheeks and a gray beard; but he did not forget his mistress, and would often speak of her with tears in his eyes, for he had not only been with her at Ava, but at Amherst he had watched her through her last illness till she died. Now he had the pleasure of seeing another Mrs. Judson; and I hope old Koochil loved her too, as she deserved to be loved.

His marriage with Mrs. Boardman made Dr. Judson very happy; and it was not long before there were again little children in his home, brothers and sisters to Georgie Boardman. Georgie Boardman, however, did not see the children as God sent them to his mother and new father, one after the other; he had been sent away to school in America. This separation from his mother had been a great grief to both her and him; but it was necessary, for boys who wish to become useful men need to learn many things, and it is not good for them to remain in heathen lands.

CHAPTER XVII.

MR. KINCAID AT RANGOON AND AVA—STORY OF PERSECUTIONS AND OF A CHRISTIAN GOVERNOR OF BASSEIN.

WE will for a time leave Dr. Judson with his loving wife and little children in their home at Maulmain, and follow some of the other missionaries who had been sent out to Burmah.

You recollect that Mr. Mason arrived at Tavoy shortly before Mr. Boardman was taken to heaven. He continued the work that had been commenced among the Karens there, and began, as I have told you, the translation of the Bible into their language. But just now, instead of going back to Tavoy, let us return to Ava and Rangoon.

Mr. Kincaid came out to Burmah the very year that Dr. Judson gave away so many tracts at the Rangoon festival. Dr. Judson had been obliged to leave Rangoon to attend to the churches in Maulmain; but the next year Mr. Kincaid was present at the festival, and great numbers of the people came to him, as they had done the year before to Dr. Judson. They had read the tracts, and Kothahbyn had been preaching in the country up the Irrawadi.

"Oh," the people said, "it is wonderful the great light that is visiting the world!"

It was like what Isaiah says: "The people that sat in darkness have seen a great light." Do you, dear children, who live always with this light around you, see it? It is quite possible to live in the light, and yet not see it; we cannot see unless our eyes are open. Pray, as David did: "Open thou mine eyes, that I may behold wondrous things out of thy law."

"How long do you intend remaining here?" a Burmese officer said to Mr. Kincaid one day.

"Until all Burmah worships the eternal God," he answered. Was not that a noble answer? He was determined that no trial, no persecution—nothing should drive him away from the work God had given him.

When he said this, I do not know that he himself expected to live till all Burmah worshipped God; perhaps he hoped it; we are taught in the Bible to hope and look for the time when, not only in Burmah, but over all the earth, God alone will be worshipped.

As more missionaries came to Rangoon, Mr. Kincaid resolved to go to Ava, for he continually heard from travellers how many were reading the tracts and inquiring about the new religion there. He packed up a large number of tracts and portions of the Bible, procured a boat, and then, accompanied by his wife, her sister, and three native Christians, started up the river towards the capital.

One of the first difficulties he experienced at Ava was, the difficulty of getting a house. The government officers did all they could to prevent him from having one. Mrs. Kincaid and her sister were British subjects, not Americans, and as soon as the officers heard this, they found them a house at once, for they were afraid of offending the English.

Mr. Kincaid found that the accounts carried to Rangoon of the numbers of inquirers at Ava were quite correct. So many flocked to the verandah of the mission house that Mr. Kincaid was often troubled; he could not talk to and teach all that came for instruction. The government officers were very polite to him, and he was invited to visit the prince Mekhara, who could speak English. The king too appeared interested in the books; not, however, on account of the religion they taught, but on account of the manner in which they were printed. Printing was new to him, and one of the printers and a printing-press were sent up to Ava, to show him how it was done.

No one hindered Mr. Kincaid at Ava; but at Rangoon sad persecutions had arisen.

One of the native Christians who had travelled to Ava with Mr. Kincaid had returned to Rangoon, and not long after he was seized, thrown into prison, beaten, loaded with chains, and compelled to hard labor. You have heard of this Christian before; it was Moung Sanlone, who had assisted Dr. Judson at the time of the Rangoon festival. He had ventured again to give away tracts in the town, and he was punished in this way because he was a

Christian, and had dared to distribute Christian books.

Moung Sanlone was even threatened with death if he did not consent to worship Gaudama instead of God; but he refused to yield, for he knew it was far better to die loving and serving God than to live serving Gaudama. He was not, however, put to death, and was even released from prison; but all his possessions were taken from him, and he was forbidden, on pain of death, to preach or distribute tracts again. Wicked men tried to prevent Moung Sanlone from serving Christ. Perhaps they thought they had succeeded, for he died soon after. But he was really only gone to serve Christ better than he had ever served him on earth. God had taken him from Burmah to that city in which we are told "his servants shall serve him."

The persecutions were not confined to Rangoon, but spread into all the districts round about, and especially into the Karen villages. Kothahbyn had for years diligently preached the gospel in these parts, and many of the inhabitants had become Christians. Now, however, they were compelled to pay very heavy taxes, and were sadly oppressed and ill-treated by the Burmese if they refused to worship Gaudama.

The consequence was, that many of the Christians moved away to find more peaceful homes elsewhere; and they carried with them the blessed knowledge they had received, and took it to other parts of the country, so that the light of the gospel spread more and more. This is not at all a new consequence of persecution. It has happened over and over and over again in the history of the church. Even as far back as the time the apostles lived we have an account of the same thing. We read that "At that time there was a great persecution against the church which was in Jerusalem, and the disciples were scattered abroad throughout the regions of Judæa and Samaria. Therefore they that were scattered abroad went everywhere preaching the word."

While these things were happening about Rangoon, there was at Ava a young Burmese nobleman who had been in the habit of visiting Mr. Kincaid in his verandah, and there had learned to love the Saviour. His sister, one of the queen's maids of honor, was very much distressed, and did all she could to persuade her brother to return to the faith of his fathers; but all her persuasions were of no avail. The only hope, she thought, would be in getting him quite away from Ava and Mr. Kincaid, to some place where he would hear nothing more of this strange religion which made him forsake the worship of Gaudama. She told her wish to the queen, and he was ordered to go to Bassein, and take the office of governor of the province.

Now Bassein is, as you may see on the map, near Rangoon; and while this young Christian grieved that he was to be sent five hundred miles from home, to a place where he expected to find no one who worshipped the true God, his heavenly Father was really sending him to help his persecuted brothers and sisters there.

One day, very soon after his arrival at Bassein, some wild-looking jungle men were brought before the new governor by the officers.

"What offence have these men committed?" he asked.

"They worship a strange God," was the answer.

"What God?"

"They call him the Eternal God."

"The Eternal God! Set the men free; let them go home in peace."

How astonished must the officers and prisoners have been! The happy Karens returned home in peace; and the news soon spread far and wide that the governor would not interfere with the Christians, for he was actually one himself. He loved the religion of Jesus, kept his day, and fulfilled his commands. If the governor would not interfere, it was of no use for the officers to do so; the persecution in Bassein was at an end; and during the two years he remained there, two thousand men and women are said to have been converted.

Kothahbyn was very active during this time among the Karens around Rangoon and all along the banks of the Irrawadi from that town to Prome. If he was persecuted in one place, he passed on to another, just as Jesus had commanded his disciples to do when he was on earth. A year or two afterwards some missionaries made a tour up the Irrawadi; and they found that in spite of fines and imprisonments and persecutions in many forms, numbers of the people were Christians, waiting to be baptized. Very many of them had had no other teacher than Kothahbyn; the glad news of salvation had been brought to them by him.

CHAPTER XVIII.

MR. KINCAID AMONG ROBBERS.

THERE were missionaries stationed at Ava, Rangoon, Amherst, Maulmain, Tavoy, and Mergui. I dare say you would think this was enough. Dr. Judson did not think so. He wrote letters to America, telling how many more missionaries were needed, and how many places there still were without teachers. Mr. Kincaid did not think so either. He remembered there were countries lying far away north of Ava, north of Burmah, to which the gospel had not yet been carried. China lay there away to the north—China, with its hundreds of millions of people. Many Chinese certainly travelled into Burmah, and some had come in contact with the missionaries. There was a Chinese convert mentioned in one of Mrs. Boardman's letters from Tavoy; but could not China itself be reached?

Mr. Kincaid thought it might be done; and besides, there were people called Shans, living to the north, who might be opened to the gospel even if China were not.

Other missionaries, Mr. and Mrs. Webb and Mr. and Mrs. Simons, had come to Ava, and could supply his place there, so Mr. Kincaid resolved to make a journey to the north. He procured a boat, and taking four native Christians with him, started up the river. The country through which he passed was very beautiful, and wide forests of teak-wood covered the sides of the hills.

At the end of three weeks Mr. Kincaid reached the city of Mogaung, which is three hundred and fifty miles from Ava. Here he stayed for a time, and took some journeys into the great plain that lay to the north towards India. It was soon evident, however, that he could go no farther, for he could get neither men nor provisions. All the people of the country appeared to be fighting against one another, and the bands of robbers that roamed about made travelling very unsafe. I do not think that the fear of robbers would have turned Mr. Kincaid back, but without men who could row the boat farther up, or food for himself and his companions, there was no choice left—he was compelled to return.

But on his way down the river, a party of banditti attacked Mr. Kincaid. Resistance was of no use; they captured him, and carried him away to their village. He was a white man, and on this account they thought him a very valuable prisoner—so valuable that twenty-five men were appointed to guard him. I suppose they thought that when his friends heard of his fate they would offer a large sum of money in order to obtain his freedom.

All the men of the band except those who had charge of Mr. Kincaid used to leave the village every morning and not return again till evening. They generally brought back with them more prisoners and a number of stolen things. As Mr. Kincaid lay bound upon the ground, he could watch the men, and see what they did with the stolen property and their prisoners. Many a time his heart sank within him at the cruelties he saw practised by those wicked men. Many of their prisoners they killed outright—all were treated most cruelly; and then the wretched men would fight and quarrel until they sank to sleep, only to prepare for more robberies the next day.

But in the mean time a difficulty arose about Mr. Kincaid. What were they to do with him? No ransom was offered for him. They did not want to keep him. They did not dare to kill him. He was a white man, and they knew that a white man's life was counted valuable, and they would surely be punished if ever it were known that they had murdered him. They were afraid, too, to release him; he had seen too much of their wrong-doings to make this safe. He might tell the government officers in some of the cities about them, and then they would be punished as surely as if they had killed him.

Here was a difficulty. They could not agree among themselves, and day after day Mr. Kincaid was kept well guarded at the village, and his captors argued about what was to be done with him. How should you like to have been Mr. Kincaid at this time, and have heard these angry men discussing whether or no they should murder you? How often his thoughts must have flown to the dear friends far away whom he might never see again. Oftener still, no doubt, he remembered the dearest Friend of all, who is never far away, but has said: "Lo, I am with you always."

Among Mr. Kincaid's guards was one face he thought he had seen before. It was the face of a young Cathay chief. Could that man ever have visited the verandah of the mission house in Ava? Had he ever stood by and listened to God's word there? It was very possible; numbers came in this way whom the missionaries never saw again. One thing was certain; this young man's behavior to the captive was very different from that of the other guards. Sometimes he gave him a kind look when he had an opportunity, and one day he managed to slip a piece of money into Mr. Kincaid's hand. "Hush!" he said, for Mr. Kincaid looked surprised, and as though he would return it; "hush, you may want it!"

Want it! Of what use could money be to him?

That evening, when the robbers returned

to the village, they brought with them as prisoner a Burmese woman. She carried a baby in her arms, and three other of her children were with her. The men wanted to know where she had hidden her property and jewels, but she would tell them nothing. In their anger at her silence, they uncovered her back, and with a heavy bamboo cane they beat her until she sank on the earth and died. Mr. Kincaid watched this sad scene with an aching heart, as he sat bound on the ground. It was the last cruelty he was to see those men commit.

In the silent night, when all were sleeping around, the young Cathayan crept to his side. He gently aroused him, unbound the cords which fastened him, and bade him go. Mr. Kincaid rose, and passed noiselessly out of the village through his sleeping guard, once more a free man. He dared not remain to thank his deliverer and urge him to forsake the wicked life he was leading, but he must often have recollected and prayed for him. I wonder what did become of that bandit; whether his companions found out who it was that had released their prisoner! And if they did, whether they ill-treated or killed him on account of it.

Mr. Kincaid was free; and after much peril and suffering he arrived at Ava. All the way he was obliged to hide by day and travel by night, and beg his food from women who came out in the early morning to draw water from the wells; for there were so many robbers prowling about it seemed hardly possible to escape them.

When at length Mr. Kincaid reached Ava, he found great changes had taken place there. There had been a civil war. The king had been dethroned by his brother, and the new monarch refused to allow the missionaries to remain. So they bade adieu to their converts and friends, and embarked for Maulmain, where they stayed for a while near Dr. Judson.

CHAPTER XIX.

LAST DAYS OF KOTHAHBYN.

WHEN the new king came into power, not only the missionaries at Ava, but also those at Rangoon, were compelled to leave, for the Christians were scattered and persecuted more than ever. They did not, however, intend to remain idle, but at once looked out for a fresh post in which to continue their work. Dr. Judson and many others were laboring at Maulmain. Dr. and Mrs. Mason were still at Tavoy. These places were under the government and protection of the good Queen Victoria, and missionaries were welcome there.

There was another strip of land lying more to the north, which was also governed by the English. This was Arracan, just separated by a range of lofty mountains from the valley where flowed the broad Irrawadi. For five years missionaries had been stationed on Ramree Island, which lies on the coast of

Arracan, but there was abundance of room for more.

To this strip of land Mr. and Mrs. Kincaid, who had left Ava, and Mr. and Mrs. Abbott, who had been living at Rangoon, resolved to go. As there were only the mountains between Arracan and the part of the land in which Ava and Rangoon were situated, they hoped that many of the poor converted Karens would make their way across, and settle again near their teachers. Mr. Abbot went to Sandoway, and Mr. Kincaid to Akyab. From Akyab it was possible to reach Ava in six or eight days. That may appear to you a long time to go so short a distance, but recollect the travelling was over steep mountain passes and through thick, rough jungle land.

Kothahbyn, of whom you have so often read, accompanied Mr. Abbott to Sandoway. He was stationed in a little village near Mr. Abbott, but it was not for long; in a few months he died. He had for several years been suffering a great deal from rheumatism, and it had sometimes been so bad that he could not get up or walk about. Now, he caught a very bad cold, and inflammation of the lungs came on. He felt he was going to die, and sent to Mr. Abbott to say he should like to come and die near him. It was the rainy season, and Mr. Abbott could not go himself to fetch the sick man, but he sent a boat, in which Kothahbyn was brought to the mission house. He was rather a troublesome patient to nurse, but Mr. Abbott was very kind, and waited upon him during the few days he lived. He did not even object if Kothahbyn called him up in the middle of the night, as he often did, saying: "Teacher, please come and rub me."

Kothahbyn was the first convert among the Karens; and ever since he had learned the love of Jesus himself he had preached to his countrymen, and great numbers had by his means been converted. He was very fond of preaching, and seemed to like nothing so well. One day, when he was in a boat with a missionary, they were nearly drowned, and Kothahbyn, on seeing the danger, exclaimed: "O teacher, I shall be drowned; I shall never preach again." The Karens were very eager to hear him too; and one time, when he was kept at home by the illness of his wife, they pressed about the house so much that there was some danger of their breaking it down. I suppose it was not very strongly built.

But even after he became a Christian, although he did so much good, he had one great fault, which was constantly giving him trouble: he was very bad-tempered. He had given way to his temper for many years—all the years that he was a child and a youth; and at last, when he desired to conquer it, although he fought very hard with it, it had grown too strong, and often conquered him instead. This sad fault frequently caused great grief to the missionaries; and yet they felt there were great excuses for him. When he was young he had no kind mother and father to point out his faults and help him to overcome them, nor did he then hear of the meek and lowly Jesus, who set us "an example that we should follow his steps."

And Kothahbyn was not talented. "Not talented and not good-tempered," you exclaim; "how could he do so much good?"

No doubt he would have done much more good if he had learned to control himself, and, as I said, that want of self-control was a constant grief and pain and trouble to himself and his friends. Solomon says: "He that hath no rule over his own spirit, is like a city that is broken down and without walls." Kothahbyn often found it so.

If he had been talented, too, he might perhaps have done more good; but I am not so sure of this. The poor Karens to whom he preached were not learned; they wanted only the simple story of a Saviour's love, and it needs very little talent to understand the words: "Jesus Christ came into the world to save sinners." Kothahbyn seems to have learned this one truth so well that his heart and head were filled with it; and when he had learned it himself he went about to his fellow-sinners, proclaiming: "Christ Jesus came into the world to save sinners."

Many people in these days are so proud that somehow they find a difficulty in understanding the easy story of Christ's love. I would rather, like Kothahbyn, get this one truth well into my head and heart, than have my head quite full of knowledge without believing this.

CHAPTER XX.

MR. ABBOTT AND MR. KINCAID AT ARRACAN—STORY OF CHETYA.

WHEN Mr. Abbott went to Sandoway, he sent two native Christians out over the mountains and into the country around, to tell the Karens that a missionary had come and would be glad to see them. They were also told to find, if possible, the young men who had been studying with Mr. Abbott at Rangoon, and ask them to come and live at Sandoway, and continue their studies there.

As soon as the news spread that the teacher had arrived, numbers flocked across the mountains to him; some to remain and study, some for books and instruction, some to escape, in a peaceful land, the persecutions to which they had been subjected.

The Burmese magistrates did all they could to prevent the Karens from moving. They set men to guard the mountain passes and turn them back; they fined them; they imprisoned them; they beat them; and yet numbers escaped and made their way to the missionaries.

You see the foolish Burmese went the wrong way to work. Suppose they had said: "Stop here, and you shall have comfortable homes; we will not tax you more than is just and right, and you shall have schools for your children, and teachers for yourselves, with liberty to worship what God you will," is it likely the Karens would have left them?

At last some of the officers did find out they were making a mistake, and that, if matters continued as they were, soon all the Karens would leave them and be settled in the English provinces; so they made things a little easier for them, and said: "Let them worship God, if they will pay the taxes and obey our laws."

Still the persecutions did not cease. In 1841, the year after he went to Sandoway, Mr. Abbott made a tour into the mountains, and met many Karens, who told him of the sufferings they had endured for reading the "White Book."

The next year came an order from the king, that the white men and their religion were to be driven out of his dominions. Now the poor Karens were persecuted afresh, and more fiercely than ever. They were seized in their huts, whole families of them, and driven away to prison. Mothers and fathers were separated from their children, and cruelly beaten unless they could give their persecutors as much money as they asked for. Children were left to starve and die without any one to nurse and care for them.

Do you wonder that now they fled across the mountains to Arracan faster than ever? They packed up all they could carry, and driving their buffaloes before them, came hungry and sad to the missionaries. Not only the missionaries, but all the British residents in the province, and Colonel Phayre, the assistant commissioner, received them kindly, and did what they could to help them. They had land on which to settle, and were supplied with food until their rice should be grown.

Happier times seemed dawning for them, but there was still another enemy they had to meet. Want and sorrow and misery often bring sickness and death with them; and so it was now. The sufferings these poor people had endured prepared other sufferings for them. In the first hot season after their arrival in Arracan, the cholera broke out among them, and destroyed many. So frightened did they become of this sad disease, that, instead of trusting in God, they ran away back to the mountains and jungles, hoping to escape, and there died of the very disease they had tried to run from, without any one to help or comfort them.

Cholera sometimes visits us also, and very sad and terrible it is when God permits it to break out anywhere; but in the East, in the cities of India and Burmah, cholera, when it sweeps over the land, is far more terrible than with us. It is an enemy here, it is an enemy there; but here and there the enemy is met in very different ways. Here, we ask God to help and deliver us, and then we set to work with hospitals and medicines, with good food, warm clothing, good nursing, and great care and cleanliness, to beat and overcome the enemy. There, fires are kindled in the streets, and kept burning night and day, which is no doubt a very good thing; and large processions of people go about the streets, beating gongs and drums and tom-toms, to frighten away the evil spirits, which, they believe, cause the disease. I should think it more likely that they frightened the sick people, and even those that were well, until it made them ill. When the cholera raged, as it often did in Rangoon, or Maulmain, or Ava, or Tavoy, the missionaries were quite worn out by attending to the sick and dying.

Mr. Abbott at Sandoway was made quite ill by his anxieties. He not only had these poor Karens to care for, but his wife and two children were taken from him to heaven; and he, too weak and sad to continue his work, was compelled to return for a time to America.

At the time that Mr. Abbott was at Sandoway, Mr. Kincaid was at Akyab. The Karens flocked to him also, coming over the mountains from the direction of Ava.

One day, a Karen chief, called Chetya, visited the white teacher. He came attended by a party of his men, and I do not know that they did much more than look about the mission station, and wonder at the strange ways of the foreigners. Mr. Kincaid told them he had God's book, which explained the way in which the true God was to be worshipped. They listened, but did not appear much interested, and soon went away to their mountains again.

Not many months after, Mr. Kincaid was surprised by receiving a letter from the mountains. Of course it did not come by post; perhaps some poor Karen brought it. It was a letter signed by Chetya and thirteen other chiefs, and its contents were to this effect. They had been considering the things which Mr. Kincaid had told them about the true God; but they were ignorant, and their people were ignorant, and they wished the teacher to come and live with them, that they might know the true God and be taught the true book. In the letter also were written the names of two hundred and seventy children who would be sent to school as soon as some one would come to teach them.

Mr. Kincaid and his fellow missionary, Mr. Stilson, prepared to go and visit these mountain tribes as soon as possible, so much had the letter pleased them. But Chetya was very impatient to receive an answer, and instead of waiting set off with a large retinue to the mission station, where he arrived before the missionaries had started. He was delighted to find the teachers preparing to visit his villages, and hastened home again to spread the intelligence, and to make preparations for the reception of his visitors. A zayat was erected by the time the missionaries arrived, in which the people assembled in order to be instructed about the true book and true God; and many little things that the rough men had noticed at the station they had done their best to provide for the use of their guests. Warm, loving hearts and eager, willing hands had worked together, and the result was great happiness and much satisfaction and pleasure.

Chetya wished much to build a house for the missionaries, and keep them altogether; but this could not be: they could not leave their posts at Akyab. They could only promise to come again on a visit, and to do their very best to find a teacher who would remain with them.

In a few years Mr. and Mrs. Kincaid were obliged to leave Arracan on account of their health, and return for a time to America. They took with them the two elder children of Mr. and Mrs. Comstock, the missionaries at Ramree.

Mr. Abbott, I told you, had lost his wife and children, and returned to America to recruit. Mr. and Mrs. Comstock also died about this time, as well as the little ones that had remained with them; so that in a very little while Mr. Stilson was the only one left of all the missionaries who had been at Arracan.

I have to tell you of the deaths of a great many persons, and you think it sad. It is sad, but you know that when Christians die they go to a better and brighter home; how bright and how glorious who can say? One by one, we must all die; and if you and I, like these servants of God, are loving and serving him, whether we die and go to Jesus, or Jesus comes for us, it will be all one: we shall only be going home.

CHAPTER XXI.

DR. JUDSON'S HOME.

I WISH I could draw you a picture of the home at Maulmain in which Dr. Judson lived so happily with his wife and little children.

In one of her letters home Mrs. Judson wrote:

"The little ones play in the verandah adjoining the room where I sit all the day with my Peguan translator. It is open to the road, and I often have inquirers. Since I commenced this letter I happened to look up, and saw a man leaning over the balustrade, looking at me very attentively. I asked him what he wanted. He replied he was looking to see me write. I immediately laid down my pen, invited him in, and he sat a long time listening to the truth. He promised to pray to the Eternal God to give him a new heart, that he might believe in the Saviour, the

Lord Jesus Christ, of whom he says he never heard till to-day. He is a Shan, who has been residing for a number of years at Pegu, and came here for trade. He lives in his boat; and while strolling about the streets was led by curiosity hither; and oh, may it be for the salvation of his soul."

I cannot tell you whether this poor Shan, who lived in his boat, did or did not become a Christian; perhaps he and Mrs. Judson have met in heaven since then. Those who do good on earth do not often know how much good they are doing. I will tell you a little story which proves that Mrs. Judson did not know all the good she was doing in the days she sat studying Peguan.

Long after she was in heaven, far away from the table at which she used to sit and write, a man came to the house to see Dr. Judson. He said he was a Christian, and wished to be baptized. He was a middle-aged, sober, respectable man, but he could not speak Burmese well. He was a Peguan from near Bangkok in Siam.

"Why do you wish to be baptized?" asked Dr. Judson.

"I believe in the Lord Jesus Christ, and I wish to enter his religion and obey his commands."

"How do you know that this is one of his commands?"

"I have read about it in the Book of Truth."

"How did you first become acquainted with the religion of Jesus?"

"Before I came to this region, a countryman of mine chanced to mention a wonderful little book which a foreign teacher at Bangkok had given him, and I had the curiosity to procure it and read it. I have never worshipped any idol since."

"Indeed! What book was it?"

"The Golden Balance."

"The Golden Balance" was a tract which Mrs. Judson had translated into the Peguan language years ago, when she used to sit there among her children with her teacher. She also translated the Pilgrim's Progress into the Burmese language; and if you had read that delightful book you know what a treat she gave to the Burmese Christians.

About this time Dr. Judson began to suffer

from cough and fever and weakness of the throat, and could no longer preach so constantly as he had been in the habit of doing. Once he was obliged to leave Mrs. Judson and the children, and try if a voyage to Calcutta, and a visit to the missionaries at Serampore would not do him good. On board the ship which took him to Calcutta Dr. Judson wrote a letter to George Boardman. Although he was far away in America, you may be sure that neither Dr. Judson nor his mother forgot him. This is part of the letter that was written on the voyage to Calcutta:

"DEAR GEORGE: I am taking a voyage for the benefit of my health, and being alone on board ship, separated from your mamma and her family, I thought I would write a few lines to you. I left her the 19th of last month, and then she was well, and Abby, Ann, Adoniram, and Elnathan. Would you like to see them all? Everybody says that Adoniram looks just like you at that age. I think there is a most striking resemblance. Elnathan has blue eyes, and looks more like his mother. I hope you will frequently pray that your brothers and sister may, as well as yourself, become partakers of Divine grace. If you get a new heart, you will, when you die, go to heaven, where your sainted father doubtless is, and where your mother and I hope to go. But if not, you will never reach our happy company, and we shall look round in vain for George. Do not forget these things, and while you are engaged in your studies take care to secure the one thing needful. Your mother and I remember you every day in our family prayers and in our secret devotions. There is nothing we so much long to hear as that you have given your heart to Jesus.

"We are glad to learn from your letters that you are happy in the family of Captain Childs. You must be very obedient and grateful for all the attentions and kindnesses you receive.

"I have had an attack of the same complaint that your own father died of; but I am deriving much benefit from the sea air. If I should recover I shall have returned to Maulmain when you receive this, and be again happy, I hope, in the society of your mamma.

"Your affectionate father,

"A. JUDSON."

Dr. Judson did return again to Maulmain, better for the change and rest he had enjoyed; and he received a warm welcome, not only from his wife and children, but from the native Christians, and his companion missionaries also.

A year after this trip to Calcutta, Dr. Judson again visited Rangoon. It was the same year that Mr. Kincaid and Mr. Abbott went to Arracan. Rangoon was, you recollect, the first place in which Dr. Judson had made his home in Burmah. It was at Rangoon he had first preached to the heathen; and though now for many years he had lived at Maulmain, he still thought of the persecuted Christians at Rangoon, and took every opportunity of going to see them.

It was a great grief to him that at Rangoon and Ava missionaries and Christians should be so ill-treated by the king and governors; and constantly he prayed that soon the days might come when all over Burmah the glorious gospel should be openly proclaimed.

Dr. Judson did not get very strong again. His friends in America asked him to return there for a time, as other missionaries had done, in order to try and recover his health; but he did not think this would be likely to benefit him, and did not wish to leave Burmah; therefore he thanked his friends, and remained where he was. His voice was too weak to allow him to preach much, so he spent more time writing and translating at home.

Because he understood the language so well, he had been many times asked to compile a dictionary. He knew this would require a great deal of time and attention, but he did not feel that it would be missionary work, and so had not undertaken it. Now, however, he commenced the dictionary, feeling sorry all the time that he was not fit for work he loved better, and which he thought might do more good. And yet, do not you think that dictionary must have been a good work, and a great help to other missionaries wishing to learn the language? How much more slowly we should get on with French or German or Latin if we had no dictionaries to help us to words.

There was a little Henry added to the number of Dr. Judson's children. It was a happy, pleasant home to which he came; a home in which the father and mother feared and loved God, and strove to teach others to do the same; a home in which the children played merrily in the verandah during the day, and at night slept soundly under their mosquito-curtains. It was not all play, though, for the children began to go to school in the mornings, and learned to read a little.

But there came a time when the little children grew pale and thin. They were ill; they could enjoy neither their food nor their play nor their lessons; and at night, instead of sleeping peacefully, they threw their fevered limbs about under the curtains, and cried and fretted in their restlessness and pain. Poor children! What could be done for them? Their mamma, too, was ill; so ill that she could not nurse them. Dr. Judson saw that if they were not all to die, he must leave Maulmain for a time, and take them out upon the broad ocean, where the cool breezes could fan their cheeks. They set sail in a ship bound for Calcutta, and as they went out to sea they all grew better. They landed near Calcutta; but as soon as they were under the influence of the heat there, they were all ill again. Dr. Judson hardly knew what to do, but he found a captain whom he had known at Maulmain, and made arrangements with him to take them all to the Isle of France.

There was one of the little family that was going another journey. While his mamma was away from him for a few days, doing some business in Calcutta, baby Henry became very ill, and not many hours after she reached him he died. They buried him in the mission burial-ground at Serampore; and with heavy hearts Dr. and Mrs. Judson left him there, and once more embarked with the other children.

Even now, when Dr. Judson had the anxiety of nursing and watching his sick wife and children, he did not forget his great determination to make Christ known wherever he went. There were sailors on board the ship which was carrying him and his family to the Isle of France. Many of them were very wicked men, but Dr. Judson had the happiness of seeing three of them become truly Christian; and twenty-three signed an agreement together, that they would endeavor to avoid sin, and try to keep God's commandments, in dependence on his strength and grace. So much good may the example of one good man do.

When the ship, after carrying them round to the Isle of France, brought them once more to Maulmain, Dr. Judson had the pleasure of seeing his wife able to work as before, and his children again playing in the verandah. Very happy they were to be in their old home, after being so long confined on shipboard.

Soon another little Henry was born to take the place of the one that had died at Serampore, and then came a little Charlie and a baby Edward. By the time baby Edward was born, all the three elder children had learned to read, and were old and steady enough to help take care of the younger ones.

While Edward was very tiny his mamma fell ill again. Dr. Judson remembered how much better she had been after her last sea voyage; and as this illness was of the same kind as that from which she had suffered before, he hoped that another voyage would restore her. The English commissioner and his wife were going to take a trip to Mergui, and they kindly asked Mrs. Judson to accompany them. She was very glad to do so, and Abby Ann and Charlie had the pleasure of being taken also.

Mrs. Judson stopped for a little while at Tavoy, which lies between Maulmain and Mergui. You remember Tavoy, and that Mrs. Judson had lived there with her first husband, Mr. Boardman, and with her children, Sarah and Georgie.

Mr. and Mrs. Mason were still at Tavoy, and very pleased indeed Mrs. Mason and Mrs. Judson were to meet again. How much they must have had to talk about! Mrs. Judson must have wanted to know all about the Karens and Burmese who had become Christians, and whether the children whom she used to teach had grown up to be good men and women. Then, too, there were old times to talk over and think about. The time when bright little Sarah died; the sad time of the revolt, when she and Mr. Boardman fled with Georgie into the town; the still sadder time of Mr. Boardman's illness; and the time of her loneliness after he was called away from her. There were the graves in the grove of trees still—she took Abby Ann with her to see them—and there, close by, was the bamboo-room which her husband had built, and to which he used to retire and pray alone. There, too, she had often prayed in days gone by; a Bible was lying on the table there still, for Mrs. Mason used the same little room when she wanted to be alone with her heavenly Father.

CHAPTER XXII.

A GRAVE AT ST. HELENA; AND A VISIT TO AMERICA.

I AM sorry to say that this voyage and the visits to Mergui and Tavoy did Mrs. Judson no good. She came back to Maulmain even weaker than when she left. If she remained in Burmah it was evident she must soon die, and leave her husband and her six dear children.

She must go home to America, the country she had left twenty years before; and as she was quite too ill to go alone, Dr. Judson must go with her. It was decided, too, that Abby Ann and her two elder brothers, Adoniram and Elnathan, should accompany their parents to America, in order to be placed at school there. As the three little ones were not yet old enough to need any schooling, it was not necessary that they should go; and they were therefore left behind with some kind missionary friends, who promised to take care of them.

I must tell you that when, with an aching heart, Mrs. Judson kissed Henry and Charlie and Edward, it was the last time their mother was ever to kiss them. This parting between mother and children is constantly happening in missionary families. Years ago Mrs. Judson had parted from her boy George; Mrs. Comstock had parted from her children; Mrs. Mason from hers; indeed, it would almost require a book by itself just to give you the names of all the missionary fathers and mothers and children who have, in different parts of the world, borne this grief for Christ's sake.

They set sail in a vessel bound for the Mauritius. By the time they arrived there, the fresh sea-breezes had so much restored Mrs. Judson that her husband hoped there was no more cause for fear, but that he might leave her to pursue her way home with the children, while he returned to his work at Maulmain and the three little boys there. This, however, he could not do; in a few days his wife was worse than ever, and he was glad to hasten her on board the vessel that was to convey them to America.

There must have been many thoughts in Mrs. Judson's mind of the dear friends she hoped so soon to see again, and above all, of her son George, who had left her a little, gentle boy, and was now a youth, sixteen years old. But it was not to see him that she was going, but to her daughter Sarah and her baby Henry, who had been growing up in the care of the angels in heaven.

The sea-breezes did not restore her; she knew soon that she should not get better. She lived until they reached the Island of St. Helena, and there she died. She was not sorry to die. When Dr. Judson spoke to her about heaven and the pleasure of seeing her Saviour there, she replied eagerly: "What can I want more?" Almost her last words were: "I ever love the Lord Jesus Christ."

She was not sorry to die; but to her husband and children her death was a great grief. They carried her body in a boat to the shore to bury it; and in that far-off island Dr. Judson found kind Christian friends who did all they could to comfort him. They took him to their houses and prayed with him, and spoke kind, loving words to him and the children. They knew he was not rich, and therefore they and the captain of the ship would not allow him to bear the expenses of the funeral; and not only did they pay this, but they made black clothes for the children, and sent them on board the ship.

How sad George Boardman must have felt when the ship reached America—the ship which he hoped would bring to him the mother from whom he had been so long separated, but which only brought the intelligence that he had no mother on earth! The sight of his sister and brothers, and of Dr. Judson, who was so kind a father to him, could not make up to him for the loss of his mother.

It was thirty-three years since Dr. Judson had left America. How many changes had taken place! He went away a young man, known only to a very few; he returned, no longer young, but he found that all who were interested in missionary work were eager to welcome him. He left, full of hope and courage and health; he returned, weak and sad, though he had hope and courage still. He left with a young wife at his side; she and her children were lying far away in a heathen land; another dear wife he had left six weeks before, sleeping in her lonely island-grave, and he had returned with three motherless children. He left with a determination to serve Christ as a missionary, and he returned with the same resolution; and though he had been in prison, as you know, and had passed through many trials and troubles, yet he did not think of settling down comfortably among his friends in America for the rest of his life; he intended to return to Burmah and his work there as soon as possible.

Dr. Judson had been rather anxious before he landed in America as to how he should procure lodgings for himself and the children; he had been absent so long that he felt almost as though he were going into a strange land. But the Christian people in America did not think of him as a stranger; they had heard of his labors for so many years; they had so often given money to support the mission stations in Burmah, and had become so interested in the reports he had sent over, that they were all ready to welcome him. He had no need to seek for lodgings; so many people wished to receive him into their houses, to show their pleasure at seeing him, and their sympathy in his sorrow, that he could not possibly visit them all.

He was asked to many missionary meetings, and was invited to speak at them. On account of the weakness in his throat he could not say much; and besides, he had spoken the Burmese language for so many years, that he did not feel quite at home with the English tongue. He disappointed the people in another way too: they wanted him to amuse them and tell them stories of what he had seen in Burmah. But he could not do it; his heart was heavy, and he was not accustomed to story-telling. He told them how much Burmah wanted help from them, and then reminded them of Christ's great love to them.

One day a lady was walking home with him, after a service at which he had spoken. She remarked that the congregation were disappointed with what he had said.

"Why, what did they want?" he asked. "I

presented the most interesting subject in the world as well as I could."

"But they wanted something different—a story."

"Well; I am sure I gave them a story—the most thrilling one that can be conceived of."

"But they had heard it before. They wanted something new from a man who had just come from the antipodes."

"Then I am glad they have it to say that a man coming from the antipodes had nothing better to tell than the wondrous story of Jesus' dying love."

CHAPTER XXIII.

The Return to Maulmain.

THE next year Dr. Judson left America again, and once more sailed for Burmah. This was in the year 1846.

He had left the three children to be taught and trained in America. But he did not go alone. Other missionaries sailed with him; but, besides these, there was with him another lady, who had become his wife, and was going to be a new mamma to the little ones in Maulmain.

When Dr. and Mrs. Judson reached Maulmain, only two of the three little boys were there. Charlie had joined his mother in heaven. The other two had by this time quite forgotten her, and were ready to love the lady that came back with their father and call her "Mamma."

Dr. Judson sent a letter to his sons in

America to tell them of his arrival in Maulmain. He says:

"I can hardly realize that I am sitting in the old house where we all lived together so long; and now your mamma, yourselves, your sister Abby Ann, and little Charlie are gone. It is now evening. I am writing in the hall where I used to sit and study when your mamma had gone down the coast with Captain and Mrs. Durand. Your new mamma has just put your little brothers, Henry and Edward, to bed. They lie in the room where you used to sleep before you removed to the corner room. Henry is singing and talking aloud to himself; and what do you think he is saying? your new mamma has just called me to listen. 'My own mamma went away, away in a boat. And then she got wings and went up. And Charlie, too, went up, and they are flying above the moon and the stars.'

"I preach in the chapel, as I used to do, but have not yet begun to work at the dictionary, for we have been very busy seeing company and getting our house and things in order. Every thing looks as it used to do when you were here. My dear boys, I don't know when I shall see you again. If I ever should, you will not be the dear little fellows I left at Worcester. But I hope, as you grow larger and change the features that are now so deeply engraven on my heart, you will also grow wiser and better, and become more worthy of my fondest love. That you will give your hearts to the Saviour is my most earnest desire. Love your dear uncle and aunt Newton. Mind all they say, and ever try to please them. I enclose a hymn that I found with Elnathan's name upon it.

"Your fond father,

"A. JUDSON."

When Dr. Judson returned he found that there were many missionaries living at Maulmain. He felt it would be better for him not to remain there, while there were so many places without missionaries at all. In Rangoon there was no missionary; they had been driven away from the town by the persecutions. Dr. Judson knew that he could not hope to preach and teach publicly in a zayat at Rangoon as he might at Maulmain; and yet he thought he might do good secretly and privately. His great work now was the dictionary. There were more clever and learned Burmese living at Rangoon than there were at Maulmain; he considered it would be a great advantage to have their help, and that if he went with this object, he should perhaps be allowed to remain unmolested.

He left his wife in Maulmain, and took a trip to Rangoon to judge for himself of the possibility of living there in peace. We will follow him in the next chapter.

CHAPTER XXIV.

"BAT CASTLE"—PERSECUTIONS IN RANGOON.

RANGOON had much altered since the time that Dr. Judson had first resided there. It was larger, there were new houses and new streets, and there were many more Englishmen and foreigners living there than formerly. Some of the streets were paved with brick, and though the work had not been done very evenly, it was an improvement to have any paving at all. It was not in such good order as Maulmain; but that will not surprise you when you recollect the different ways in which the two towns were governed.

The government at Rangoon was as bad as ever, or even worse, as I will tell you. The wonder to me is that any foreigners, and especially any Englishmen, would live in such a town, except as Dr. Judson did, with the hope of making it better. Those who did reside there were mostly merchants, who traded in the products of the country and made money by them, or captains and sailors, who attended to the shipping of goods, and stayed at the port between their voyages.

Dr. Judson had some difficulty in finding a house; and after hunting for something better, he took the upper story of an old brick house in a street called the Mussulman-street. He returned to Maulmain for his wife and children and some of his furniture; but he decided to leave a great many things behind, for it was impossible to say how soon he might be compelled to move again; and the custom-house officers taxed so many things that it was a great deal of trouble to take them.

The first news, however, that reached them after their arrival at Rangoon was that the house in Maulmain, where they had left their goods, was burnt to the ground, and every thing had been destroyed. This was a great loss, for Dr. Judson was not rich, and had he been, there was not a possibility of replacing the things that were burnt, for many of them were presents from kind friends in America. Dr. Judson, however, was not the worst sufferer by this fire. Mr. Stevens, one of the missionaries, with his wife and children, were living in the house; they were aroused from their slumbers in the middle of the night, and only escaped with their lives. It was believed that some wicked person had set fire to the house on purpose.

The brick house at Rangoon, Mrs. Judson called "Bat Castle." I think from the description she gives of it it quite deserved the name. The rooms were very large, but there were no glass windows, only holes in the walls, which might, if needful, be covered with wooden shutters. Along the low ceilings ran large beams, and on the tops of these beams great numbers of bats hid themselves by day, and at night they flew about the rooms, making a loud noise.

The bats were not the only inhabitants of the house which Dr. and Mrs. Judson would rather have been without. Large numbers of sparrows swarmed about the beams, also, and Mrs. Judson speaks of beetles, spiders, cockroaches, lizards, rats, ants, and mosquitoes.

In a letter which she wrote to a friend in America, she said that though only one cockroach had paid her a visit since she commenced writing, about twenty large ants had crossed her paper. I am afraid our letters would not be very steadily written if we had such unpleasant visitors.

Dr. Judson worked industriously at his dictionary, and privately sent out one or two native converts, who had come with him, to tell any Christians they might meet with where to find him.

There were very few Christians at that time in the Rangoon province; all who could do so had gone away, for the vice-governor, or raywoon, who had all the power in his own hands, was a very bloodthirsty man. He hated Christians, and was so cruel that it is said his house and courtyard resounded day and night with the cries of the people who were being tortured there. No wonder the Christians were afraid to come in his way. Dr. Judson could not even give away a tract in public, not only on account of the danger to himself, but no one would have been found bold enough to receive it.

In spite, however, of all this fear, a few Christians used to meet on Sunday mornings at "Bat Castle." They were afraid of being noticed, and not many of them would venture to walk up to the house in their own dress as though they were going to visit Dr. Judson. A few did—these were the boldest; the rest came one by one, some carrying parcels, as though they were porters only going there on business; others with baskets of fruit upon their heads, dressed as servants, as though they were on their way home from market, where they had been to procure provisions for the family. When they were all assembled, the doors were barred, and there in secret they prayed and read God's word together.

At the same beautiful reservoir where, so many years before, Dr. Judson had baptized the first Burmese convert, he had the pleasure of once more baptizing. Now, as then, it was after sunset, for fear of the enemy. It was a young man who was baptized that June evening, a son of one of the oldest native Christians, who lived at a village a little distance from Rangoon.

The next morning, as the young convert was returning home, his heart full of happy thoughts, he met his father in the hands of some officers. He had been taken prisoner, and was being conveyed to the court of the governor for examination. You will be glad to hear that it was not to the court of the raywoon he was going; and the old viceroy had given Dr. Judson a promise that he would not interfere with the Christians. The young man returned to Rangoon with his father, full of grief and sorrow. Some of the Christians brought the intelligence to Dr. Judson, and all waited in fear and anxiety to know the result.

The old man was taken into the court to the officer who had sent the order for his arrest.

"Why have you brought the man before me?" asked the officer.

"He is accused of heresy, and of frequenting the house of Jesus Christ's teacher," was the reply.

"On what authority?"

"Here is your written order.'

"My written order! What? Where? I

have given no order. It must be one of my clerks. It must be a mistake. Go about your business."

"I thought it strange," said the old man, "that you should summon me on a charge of heresy, as it is well known that I worship the true God."

"God!" said the officer; "worship any god you like; if you villagers pay your taxes, what more do we want with you?"

Now the fact was, this officer had written the order; but after he had done so, he had told the viceroy of it, and had found that he was not pleased. Therefore it was that this Christian was released.

The Sunday after this occurrence no one ventured to the upper room in Dr. Judson's house where they had met for worship. The meetings in Mussulman-street were known, and had been remarked upon in the government house; and though this old man had been released, it did not follow that others would escape so easily. Many had met with martyrdom for Christ's sake in Rangoon; and one man, Mau Ya, after he had been fined and whipped and sentenced to death, had been made a pagoda slave. This was considered the worst kind of slavery. Colonel Burney begged, as a great favor, that Mau Ya might be set at liberty, and at last the governor yielded.

It was not long before accounts of the coming and going at Dr. Judson's house were carried to the bloodthirsty raywoon himself. He at once set guards in the street to watch and seize any one going in or out who was not known to be a servant belonging to the family. Some one of Dr. Judson's trusty friends apprised him of the danger. But what was to be done? It was Saturday, and the next morning any one who came to the service would be taken prisoner and carried before the vice-governor. Not a moment must be lost.

Dr. Judson despatched his two native assistants at once, by different roads, to call upon all the Christians and warn them not to come. Unfortunately, four young Karens were in the house. They could not remain there, and yet how could they escape? Dr. Judson contrived to get the key of the outer gate from the landlord that night; in the darkness he quietly let them out of the house; they made haste from the town, and by morning were far on the way to their native jungle.

And so it came to pass that the cruel raywoon's guard was set in vain. Dr. and Mrs. Judson prayed and watched in some anxiety. They could not tell whether their messengers had succeeded in their errand, for they had not returned; but no one approached the house; all was quiet. Had they not reason to sing, "The Lord is on my side; I will not fear: what can man do unto me? The Lord taketh my part with them that help me. It is better to trust in the Lord than to put confidence in man. It is better to trust in the Lord than to put confidence in princes."

I suppose, as no one came to the house that Sunday morning, the guard did not think it necessary to watch so very closely in future, for Christians and inquirers did still find their way there. But how alarmed they were lest it should be known! They were even afraid to take a book from Dr. Judson in his own house. Yet so much did they want books and tracts that, as they went out, they would snatch one hastily from a box near the door, and hide it under their dress. They doubtless guessed that their kind teacher had placed the box of books there on purpose that they might do this.

In the midst of all this trouble came the rainy season and the great Buddhist fast. The Lent fast, which the Buddhists keep, continues about four months.

This year the vice-governor ordered that during the whole time neither flesh nor fowl should be sold in the bazaars, and compelled foreigners as well as natives to keep the fast. The only baker in the town went away, and Mrs. Judson had nothing in the house with which to make bread. They could still procure milk, but it was buffalo's milk, and far from good; almost the only things left to eat were rice and fruit.

The children became ill, partly in consequence of the dampness; then fruit was not good for them, and they grew tired of the constant rice, and longed for something different. Mrs. Judson, too, was ill, and grew so weak that she was at last unable to sit up; then Dr. Judson also fell ill, and for six weeks could do nothing.

One day during this dreary time Mrs. Judson tells us they had a very good dinner.

"You must contrive to get something which mamma can eat; she will starve to death," Dr. Judson said one morning to his man, who was going to the bazaar to see what could be procured.

"What shall I get?"

"Any thing."

"Any thing?"

The man went. He returned bringing something with him; it was cooked and sent up to table. How nice that stew was! How Henry and Edward and their mamma enjoyed picking those little bones! But what bones were they?

Henry thought it was touktah, a kind of lizard which is sometimes eaten; but he was mistaken. The cook was asked what animal it was. He certainly looked as though he knew, but he said he did not.

"What did we have for dinner to-day?" they asked in the evening of the man who had bought for them.

"Were they good?"

"Yes, excellent. What were they?"

"Rats," was the answer.

He had bought them in a Chinese shop. The Chinese eat rats; but I wonder whether Mrs. Judson would have done so had she known in time what her cook was preparing.

Another supply of food Dr. Judson procured was fifty fowls, which he managed to buy from a Mussulman. They were small and lean, and would doubtless prove tough, very unlike those we see in our poulterers' shops; but there they were, all clacking and crowing, and promising a supply of food for weeks to come. Twenty of these precious fowls were stolen the very first night, and eight more the man who had sold them borrowed back; so that more than half disappeared at once. The remainder were killed and eaten as they were wanted. It was of no use saving them to be either stolen or borrowed.

A box of biscuits was also sent by some kind friend in Maulmain; and in course of time this trouble came to an end, and Dr. and Mrs. Judson and the children all grew better.

In the autumn they returned to Maulmain; but this was not because they were afraid of hardships; they were both willing to suffer for Christ's sake; but circumstances made it impossible for them to remain longer at Rangoon.

CHAPTER XXV.

NATIVE PREACHERS—STORY OF MYAT KYAN.

FROM the time when first the Burmese and Karens had begun to receive the gospel, many of those who had become Christians had devoted their lives to spread the good news among their countrymen. This had been a very great assistance to the missionaries, and God had very greatly blessed the labors of these native teachers.

It would be quite impossible to tell you of all these good and devoted men; it is only a few even of the white missionaries of whom you have heard.

You remember the Karen Kothahbyn, who was sold as a slave for being in debt. He was ransomed by the missionaries, taken into Dr. Judson's family, and there had learned how Jesus too had ransomed him. He preached to thousands of Karens, as you have heard, and died at Sandoway, in Arracan, to which place he accompanied Mr. Abbott.

Moung Ing, too, one of the first Rangoon converts, you recollect. He had been at Ava during the time of Dr. Judson's imprisonment; afterwards you heard of him at Tavoy, helping Mr. Boardman in his last illness: and then at Mergui, where he died.

Moung Salone, who was so persecuted at Rangoon, you have not forgotten; and Ko Eu, who was imprisoned for giving away books at Rangoon. He was at this time still busy preaching Christ, and so was Mau Ya, who had been made a pagoda slave; and many others, not only in Maulmain and Tavoy, but even in Rangoon, Bassein, and the districts around, were engaged in the same work.

When Dr. Judson returned to Maulmain he received a welcome from an old man who had known him many years. I do not mean Mr. Wade, though he doubtless welcomed his friend warmly, and as years passed on neither he nor Dr. Judson were young any more.

The person of whom I speak was a Karen pastor named Myat Kyan. Though old and

poor and blind now, he was a very well-educated and intelligent man. He had been brought up a Buddhist: but he had become dissatisfied with the religion of Gaudama long before he had heard of the religion of Jesus. From the Karens he had become acquainted with their traditions of an eternal God, the Creator of all things, and he longed to discover the truth about him.

You have heard of the Brahmins in India, and the cruelties they sometimes practise on themselves in order to become holy. There are Brahmins also in Burmah, and for two or three years Myat Kyan joined one, who undertook to instruct him. He lived away from his friends with this Brahmin, denied himself all comforts, and tried constantly to become more and more devout and holy. But he found that neither he nor his teacher became any better than other men, and, disappointed and disgusted, he left him and returned home.

There are also Mohammedans in Burmah. One day Myat Kyan entered a Mohammedan mosque. There he heard, "There is one God, and Mohammed is his prophet." The idea of one God was not new to him; he was glad to hear it again; but what he learned of Mohammed his prophet did not satisfy him.

Next he went to the Roman-catholics. From them he heard of Christ, the Saviour of the world; but when he found that Roman-catholics worshipped a woman, he thought their religion worse than the religion of Gaudama, for Gaudama was at least a man.

Myat Kyan left Rangoon and settled at Maulmain much about the same time that Dr. Judson and Mr. Wade removed there. Indeed, it was the war during which Dr. Judson had been imprisoned which caused Myat Kyan and his family to leave Rangoon.

I think God must have been leading this poor Burman, who so much wanted to know the truth, for he took a house very near the zayat in which Dr. Judson preached. He was not long in making his way there. Happy man! there he found what he wanted; for he found Christ, a man and yet God. Day after day, from morning till evening, he was at the zayat; he had been very thirsty, but now he went to Jesus to drink.

When his brother and his wife and sons discovered that Myat Kyan had become a

Christian, they were extremely angry. His brother said he would disown him, and his wife that she would separate from him, and his sons said that they would never more call him father. But Myat Kyan had heard and believed the words, "He that loveth wife or children more than me, is not worthy of me;" and rather than give up the dear Saviour whom he had so long wanted, and had at last found, he decided to give up all that was dearest to him on earth.

You will be glad to hear that, in course of time, his wife and one of his own sons, as well an adopted son, not only were once more friendly to him, but themselves became Christians.

Myat Kyan devoted himself to helping the missionaries. Although a man who held a good position himself, he was never ashamed to sit down in the zayat by the side of a poor beggar-woman, and try to explain to her the true way to become rich. He it was who induced the missionaries to visit the Karen villages of Dong-yahn; for he used to say to them, "The Karens are not like the Buddhists; they have no idols and no priests; and if the teachers would go and preach to them, great numbers would listen and believe."

He was with Mr. Wade when the missionaries first went to Dong-yahn, and he steered the boat up the river for them. Indeed, for many years he was in the habit of accompanying them in their tours; and if at any time the boat stopped, as it often did, on account of the tide or in order that the cooking might be done, Myat Kyan would disappear among the bushes. Why? He had gone away to pray; for he loved prayer, and sometimes prayed alone all night long.

When he became old he also became blind; but still he would go to the zayat, led by a little child, and preach. He was poor too, for long ago he had given up his business to become an assistant to the missionaries. Mr. Wade was grieved to see him in want, and did all he could to help him, for he loved his old friend; but missionaries are not rich in this world's goods.

Myat Kyan would have had more for himself if he had not given so much away. Once his wife said to him, "We are so poor, we had better keep this money for ourselves." But he answered: "I can manage with less to eat, but I must give what I can for Christ's sake." Do you think this was foolish? Surely Christ did not think so. When he comes with his holy angels in glory, and separates the sheep from the goats, do you not think he will say to Myat Kyan: "Inasmuch as ye did it unto one of the least of these my brethren, ye did it unto me. Come ye blessed of my Father, inherit the kingdom prepared for you."

Poor, old, blind Myat Kyan may be counted a rich and happy man. He was alive at the time of which we are writing, and lived for a few years longer; but in the year 1852 the cholera swept over the land and carried Myat Kyan and many other Christians from Burmah away to heaven.

CHAPTER XXVI.

Martyrdom of Thagua.*

THE following account of the martyrdom of one of the Karen pastors was written in Burmese by a Burmese doctor, an eye-witness and a heathen.

Thagua, pastor of the White Book people in the vicinity of Bassein, was taken by the Burman magistrate on the accusation of having called in the English to take their country. They seized him and his son, and struck him thirty lashes on his way to prison. The son they struck twenty-five lashes. A nephew also was beaten. They took him to the governor and paid thirty rupees to the ruler.

Now these Burmans were agreed in killing all the disciples, but waited a little to get money. They said to the governor: "These White Book men will come and kill you, as

* From "The Gospel in Burmah," by Mrs. Wylies.

they did the chiefs in Rangoon." The governor then said: "Seize them."

So they seized the pastor and forty of his people, and hooked them together with iron hooks. Then they liberated the old men, and told them to go and get one hundred and thirty rupees,* and they should be free again. The elders did so, and paid the hundred and thirty rupees; but the Burman Kala did not free them, but hooked them again.

The next day he dragged out Thagua, the pastor, and struck him twice, then pressed him between bamboos, then tied him by the neck into a mango-tree, his hands tied behind to the trunk of the tree. Thagua cried out:

"My lord, my lord, do you kill me?"

Kala answered: "Give me a hundred and seventy rupees, and you shall be free."

Thagua replied: "I have no silver, my lord."

The magistrate answered: "The disciples give you a hundred rupees a year."

"No, my lord, they never gave me so much."

Then said Kala to the disciples: "Give his

* The value of a rupee is about fifty cents.

ransom, and take your leader, and all shall be peace. If not, we will slaughter him."

The disciples said: "My lord, if his life may be spared we will give the money."

The hundred and seventy rupees were given, but still they did not free him. Then Kala led them all back to the village of Pataw, and gave the pastor into the hands of the judge. The judge reviled him, saying:

"If your God is almighty, bid him take you out of these hooks."

Thagua replied: "If the eternal God does not now save me from your hands, he will save me eternally in the world to come."

The judge asked: "How do you know that?"

Thagua replied: "God's holy book tells me so; and it is true."

The judge replied: "Yes, you teach the people this book, and because you are talented and cunning, the white men come and take our country."

Then the judge himself fell upon him, mad with rage, and beat him with the elbow severely. Then hooked him with five pairs of hooks, and ordered him back to prison.

Three days after the judge again dragged up Thagua and said: "Your God, you say, can save you. Read his book before me now."

Thagua replied: "Though I read, you will not believe, but persecute me still. But the eternal God, my Judge and your Judge—the Lord Jesus Christ—he will save me."

"Command him then to save you from my hands now," said the Burman.

The chief judge then beat him with a cudgel as large as his wrist thirty blows, then ordered him back to prison with very little rice.

Two days after Kala went to this judge, and Thagua asked him: "My lord, what do you?"

"Kill you every one," he replied, and kicked him as a horse kicks.

Then said Thagua: "We cannot live," and dropped his head.

Then said Kala to the judge: "Kill these men, and I will give you a viss of silver."

"If I kill them, I cannot endure the punishment," said the judge; but he took the silver.

A day or two after, Kala went and gave him

fifty rupees more; but the judge said: "If you will marry your daughter to my son, I will kill them."

Then Kala replied: "Brother, I will marry them."

Then the judge said: "If I do not destroy them, the white people will come and take our lands, and kill us every one."

Then he scourged Pastor Thagua three times.

Thagua said: "If because I worship God you torture me, kill me at once, I entreat you."

Then they took him, struck him sixty times, fastened him to a cross, shot him, and cut him in three pieces.

Is not this a sad story? Do you not wish that the white foreigners would indeed come, and set the persecuted Christians free? They were coming; but we must go back a little in the story, to the time when Dr. Judson left Rangoon and returned to Maulmain.

CHAPTER XXVII.

Dr. Judson's Last Voyage.

THE day was coming when Rangoon and Bassein, and all Pegu, was to be freed from the cruel oppressors who now held sway there; but Dr. Judson was not to remain on earth to see it. His work here was nearly done. The dictionary was not complete, but God could provide some one else to do that; Burmah had not become a Christian country; but the preaching of the gospel he must quite leave to others now.

One night Dr. Judson arose from bed to attend to one of the children, who had been suddenly taken ill. The night was damp and chilly; he took cold from the exposure, and the cold brought on fever. He had often suffered from fever before; but this time he was worse than usual, and the remedies which were resorted to did not cure him.

Mrs. Judson wrote a letter to the children in America, telling them of their papa's illness; and as this letter is very interesting, and gives a better account than I could write, I have copied it for you.

"MY VERY DEAR CHILDREN: I have painful news to tell you—news that I am sure will make your hearts ache; but I hope our heavenly Father will help you to bear it. Your dear papa is very, very ill indeed; so much so that the best judges fear he will never be better. He began to fail about five months ago, and has declined so gradually that we were not fully aware of his danger until lately; but within a few weeks those who love him have become very much alarmed.

"In January we went down to Mergui by the steamer, and when we returned, thought he was a little better; but he soon failed again. We next spent a month at Amherst; but he received but little, if any benefit. Next the doctors pronounced our house—the one you used to live in—unhealthy, and we removed to another. But all was of no use. Your dear papa continued to fail till suddenly, one evening, his muscular strength gave way, and he was prostrated on the bed, unable to help himself. This occurred about two weeks ago.

"The doctor now became alarmed, and said the only hope for him was in a long voyage. It was very hard to think of such a thing in his reduced state, particularly as I could not go with him; but after we had wept and prayed over it one day and night, we concluded it was our duty to use the only means which God had left us, however painful.

"We immediately engaged his passage aboard a French bark bound for the Mauritius; but before it sailed he had become so very low that no one thought it right for him to go alone. They therefore called a meeting of the mission, and appointed Mr. Ranney, the superintendent of the press, to accompany him. It was a great relief to me, for he is a very kind man, and loves your dear papa very much; and he will do every thing that can be done for his comfort. The officers of the vessel, too, seemed greatly interested for him, as did every one else.

"He was carried on board a week ago yesterday in a litter, and placed on a nice easy cot made purposely for him. I stayed on board with him all day, and at dark came home to stay with the children. The next day I found that the vessel had only dropped down a little distance, and so I took a boat and followed. I expected this would certainly be the last day with him; but it was not. Friday I went again; and though he did not appear as well as on the previous days, I was forced to take, as I then supposed, a final leave of him.

"But when morning came, I felt as though I could not live throughout the day without knowing how he was. So I took a boat again, and reached the vessel about two o'clock P. M. He could not speak, except in whispers, but seemed very glad that I came. The natives that I had sent to fan him till he should get out of the river came to me, and begged to have him taken ashore again; and so small was my hope of his recovery, that my heart pleaded on their side, though I still thought it duty to do as the doctor had ordered. I came away at dark, and though his lips moved to say some word of farewell, they made no sound. I hope that you, my dear boys, will never have cause to know what a heavy heart I bore back to my desolate home that night.

"The vessel got out to sea about four o'clock on Monday, and last night the natives returned, bringing a letter from Mr. Ranney. Your precious papa had revived again, spoke aloud, took a little tea and toast, said there was something animating in the touch of the sea-breeze, and directed Mr. Ranney to write to me that he had a strong belief it was the will of God to restore him again to health. I feel somewhat encouraged, but dare not hope too much.

"And now, my dear children, it will be three, perhaps four long months before we can hear from our loved one again, and we shall all be very anxious. All that we can do is, to commit him to the care of our heavenly Father; and if we never see him again in this world, pray that we may be prepared to meet him in heaven.

"Your most affectionate Mamma,

"EMILY C. JUDSON."

It was a sad account to send to the poor children in America, was it not? It was sad, too, for Mrs. Judson; she would have accompanied her husband, but in truth she too was ill, and soon after they parted she was so much worse that it was a good thing she was not with him, for she could not have done any thing for him, and wanted nursing herself.

Dr. and Mrs. Judson knew when they parted that they should probably never see each other again until they met in heaven; and they had talked together about it, with aching hearts indeed, but without fear. One day Mrs. Judson said to her husband—it was a little while before he was carried to the ship:

"It is the opinion of most of the missionaries that you will not recover."

"I know it," he answered; "but no man ever left this world with more inviting prospects, with brighter hopes, or warmer feelings;" and he burst into tears.

But why did he weep? because he feared death?

"No," he said; "it is not because I shrink from death that I wish to live; but a few years would not be missed from my eternity of bliss, and I can well afford to spare them, both for your sake, and for the sake of the poor Burmese. I am not tired of my work, neither am

I tired of the world; yet when Christ calls me home, I shall go with the gladness of a boy bounding away from school."

"Then death would not take you by surprise," said Mrs. Judson, "if it should come even before you could get on board ship?"

"Oh, no," he said; "death will never take me by surprise—do not be afraid of that. I feel so strong in Christ. He has not led me so tenderly thus far to forsake me at the very gate of heaven. No, no; I am willing to live a few years longer, if it should be so ordered; and if otherwise, I am willing and glad to die now."

The native Christians did not at all like the thought of their beloved teacher going to sea so ill as he was, and as you have heard, begged Mrs. Judson to have him brought back even after he was on board the ship. Ko Eu was one of those who accompanied him on board the ship and returned with the pilot.

The captain of the vessel was very kind, and though he could not speak English, he did all in his power to show his sympathy for the sick missionary and his friends. But neither the kindness of the captain and Mr. Ranney nor the sea-breezes from which so much had been hoped could do any good.

A week passed away, and then there came a day when Mr. Ranney and the native servant Panapah stood by Dr. Judson's bedside to see him die.

The officers on board gathered in sorrow around the cabin-door and watched the sad scene—poor Panapah weeping bitterly; Mr. Ranney by the bedside holding the much-loved hand in his; while the breathing of the dying missionary grew softer and fainter until it ceased altogether, and he was gone home to his Saviour.

His body was buried in the broad, deep ocean, far away from those who had loved him on earth. But God's eye knows where his servant's sleeping dust is lying; and the day is coming when, at the voice of the Son of God, "the sea shall give up the dead which are in it;" and then Dr. Judson, and all those who have been the means of turning many to righteousness here, shall come forth to the resurrection of the just, and shine as the stars for ever and ever.

The letter containing the intelligence of

his illness was as yet hardly on its way to his children in America; and they were happy and all unconscious of their loss for weeks and months after they were orphans. And not only they; the ship did not return to Maulmain, but was obliged to continue its course to the Mauritius; so that in the zayats of Burmah, and in the homes of the missionaries and of the native Christians, and in that one home where his presence was most of all missed, prayers were put up to God day after day for his recovery and safe return.

It was three months before Mr. Ranney and Panapah returned to Maulmain with the intelligence of how soon Dr. Judson's sufferings had ended. I need not tell you about the grief felt there, and at all the other mission stations in Burmah. Mrs. Judson and the children left, and returned to America as soon as an opportunity presented itself; she was far from strong; and now she is in the better land, where the inhabitants no more say they are sick.

CHAPTER XXVIII.

THE DISPENSARY AT RANGOON.

IT was in the year 1850 that Dr. Judson died. In 1851 Mr. Kincaid returned from America; and he, with Dr. Dawson, went to Rangoon, dark though the prospect was there.

They hoped to gain permission from the king himself to remain, and then they need not fear the cruel raywoon. They sent a messenger to Ava, and while he was absent they determined to do what they could in spite of the governor.

They took medicines with them, and opened a dispensary. By this means they tried to do good to the bodies of those who came to them, and at the same time took the opportunity of pointing out to them the way of life—the way to the great Healer, and to the land in which which there is no pain. Many people were very glad to come for medicine, but oh how afraid they were of the cruel governor. And do you wonder, when you recollect that even in passing by his house they could distinctly hear the groans of those who were being tortured in the courtyard?

Why he did not at once capture the missionaries I do not know. Perhaps he thought that as this messenger was gone to Ava, he had better wait until the king sent a reply to their request; perhaps, too, he saw they were known to a great many foreigners in the town; and as already there was some reason to fear that his cruelties to English subjects had come to the ears of the English governors of India, he might have felt afraid of the consequences if more provocation was given.

He did all he could, however, to hinder and annoy them. Though not in prison, Mr. Kincaid was declared a prisoner, and was forbidden to walk beyond his own house without a Burmese officer to go with him, to watch where he went and listen to what he said. This must have been very uncomfortable, and I should think that Mr. Kincaid stopped at home a good deal.

In a month or two, however, a message

came from the king—a very kind and polite message, bidding them welcome to Rangoon, and saying he hoped they would remain. The governor then dared not interfere very much, and the people were no more afraid to visit the mission house. The Karen Christians flocked in from the country round, and sad tales of persecution and cruelty they brought—tales like that one I have given you of the martyrdom of Thagua, the Bassein pastor. It was about this time he was put to death. The hearts of the missionaries were filled with grief on account of the sufferings of the people, and they prayed constantly that brighter days might soon dawn.

One day one of the chief pongyees called at the mission house with some young priests, his pupils. Ko Eu, who was with the missionaries, was about to preach a sermon when this priest arrived. He was asked to sit down with the other people and listen to what was said. He answered that he did not wish to do so, but said that if Dr. Dawson would allow his pupils to remain, he would wait for them below. A Bible was handed to him, and while the young men listened to Ko

Eu, their teacher sat down and read God's word.

When the service was over, Dr. Dawson went down to speak to the pongyee. He had been so much interested in his book that he asked permission to keep it. The missionaries had been forbidden by the governor to give away books; and Dr. Dawson was sorry to say he could not grant the request. He told his visitor that he was welcome to sit and read as long as he pleased. A volume of tracts was lying on a mat near the priest, which he also looked at, and this he asked to borrow, as there were some things in it he wished to copy.

"Certainly," Dr. Dawson said; "it was a pleasure to lend the book."

The pongyee appeared much gratified; he rolled the book carefully in a handkerchief, and handed it to one of the attendants to carry home for him. Then he politely asked Dr. Dawson to visit his kyoung, and took his leave.

Shortly after Dr. Dawson did pay a visit to a kyoung, in order to see a priest who was ill.

One of the young men was sent to the mission house to conduct him. Their road lay round the base of the great Shway Dagon pagoda—the same way that Dr. and Mrs. Judson had been in the habit of going every morning so many years before, when they used to bathe in the reservoir, until the order came to prevent their taking that road. Dr. Dawson passed those tanks of water, and walked on into a beautiful grove of trees—jack, mango, and palm.

In this grove the kyoung was situated. Dr. Dawson ascended the steps and entered a large hall. At the farther end, upon a cushion, sat the sick pongyee. Behind him was a screen, which hid from view a number of idols, tiny pagodas, and gilt boxes containing sacred books and other things of that kind.

When the pongyee had described his symptoms to the doctor, and had been advised what to do for his health, he asked a great many questions about the cities and towns, the manners and customs of the people in the "big island of America." Dr. Dawson tried to explain to him that America was not an island, but a continent, and told him what a continent was.

The priest was very interested in all that

he heard, and was particularly pleased when Dr. Dawson told him what a hospital was, and described to him the large, clean rooms, with their rows of neat, comfortable beds. It was quite new to him to hear how carefully the sick were tended, of the skilful doctors who daily visited them, the kind and watchful nurses who waited upon them, the visitors who came to comfort and cheer them, and how many of them, instead of dying from want of care, recovered their health and strength, and returned home able to work and provide for themselves again.

The pongyee saw there was a great difference between America and his own country. "But," said he, "after all, our religion is not so very different from yours."

"Not different! Oh, yes," answered Dr. Dawson; "there is all the difference in the world; as much difference as there is between midday and midnight. Why, how many gods have you?"

"A great many."

"Your books say there are twenty-eight."

"Yes, we have a great many, but not so many as the Brahmins; they have millions."

"And where are all your gods?"

"Some are in other worlds, some are gone to nigban." That is, gone out of existence altogether.

"And how many gods have you had in this world?"

"We have had four already, and one is yet to come."

"Well, the Christian religion teaches us that there is but one God, who is without beginning or end. He is never sick, and can never grow old nor die as your gods do. Are you the head of this kyoung?"

"Yes."

"And the young men obey you?"

"Yes."

"But suppose the college had fifty heads, what then? You would tell your pupils to do one thing, another pongyee would tell them to do something else, until they might be told to do fifty different things at once. How would you get on?"

"That would be a bad business; we should be all in confusion."

The pongyee saw that not only a college, but a world, governed in this way, would be very badly governed; but he did not like to say any thing more about it; he still wished to believe in his many gods.

"Our rule," he said, is this: "Do good, and you will get good; do evil, and you will get evil. We ought to feed the poor, to give medicines to the sick, to build kyoungs for the priests, and to make offerings in our temples. If we do this, we shall receive honor from the gods."

"Christ's religion," replied Dr. Dawson, "teaches us also to do good; but it teaches us too that we are his servants, and must obey him. If a servant obeys his master, who has the honor?"

"The master," answered the priest; "for it is only the duty of the servant; there is no praise due to him."

"So when we do what Christ bids us, the honor is his, not ours. He tells us to do all to his glory, and when we have done all, to say, 'We are unprofitable servants; we have done that which is our duty to do.' There is a great difference in all this between our religion and yours."

In this way the missionaries talked, even

with the priests. Dr. Dawson at length rose, and bidding farewell to his patient, returned home through the mango grove and around the base of the great pagoda. No doubt as he went he prayed the prayer that Jesus taught us: "Thy kingdom come. Thy will be done: as in heaven, so on earth." It is in fact a prayer that all men may become the servants of God; and it is a prayer that will be most surely answered, for God has promised it.

CHAPTER XXIX.

HOW THE PERSECUTIONS IN PEGU WERE ENDED BY ITS ANNEXATION TO BRITISH INDIA.

ONE Sunday afternoon at the end of the month of November, 1851, a report spread through the town of Rangoon that an English steamer was coming up the river, and that three men-of-war were waiting at the mouth. The very possibility of such a thing alarmed the wicked raywoon; and he sent off, one after the other, two boats full of men to look for the ships, and see if the report was really true.

He had cause enough to be alarmed, for he knew that not only had he ill-used the subjects of the king of Burmah, but that many English and other foreigners had been most cruelly treated, and some had even been put to death by him. By-and-by the boats were seen returning. Crowds of people waited for them on the river banks. Was the report true? Were there really English war-ships in the river? Yes; the messengers had seen two armed steamers measuring the waters in the river, and putting down buoys. They were not alone, but were towing up a war-ship with fifty guns.

The town was thrown into a great excitement by this confirmation of the report. The raywoon despatched messengers to inform the king, and began at once to collect soldiers and arm them as well as he could. He had nothing better than rusty old muskets to give them, however; and the large guns in the town were not worth much. Such cannon as there were were taken up to the Shway Dagon height, and men were busy dragging them up the greater part of the night. This pagoda hill was turned into a kind of fortress; and here any one who had treasures to preserve carried them for safety. The wicked governor did not know what to do; he seemed to be at his wit's end. He declared that if the English attempted to land he would at once set fire to the town, and kill all the foreigners who lived in it; and he gave orders that any one, whether foreigner or native, who went to the river bank, should be beheaded.

The missionaries, as they dared not go to the shore, watched the approach of the vessels from the roof of their house, from which they could very well see the broad Irrawadi. They saw a boat put off from one of the steamers and come to the shore. Commodore Lambert, who was in command of the expedition, had sent a message to the governor. It was only a message to ask at what time to-morrow it would be convenient to the governor to receive a communication from the commodore. So frightened was the governor, and so anxious to put off the evil day, that he sent back an answer to the effect that to-morrow would not be convenient at all; the commodore must wait till the next day. The commodore was quite willing to wait; so all day Wednesday, as on Monday and Tuesday, the preparations for defending Rangoon were continued.

While Commodore Lambert waited the raywoon's convenience, he sent Captain Latter to ask Mr. Kincaid to come to him. Mr. Kincaid was not sorry to go; and for two hours he talked with the commodore of all the cruelties which the wretched governor had perpetrated. The expedition had been sent to make inquiries about two Englishmen—Captain Shepherd and Captain Lewis; for the governor-general of India had heard that they had been ill-treated in Rangoon. But now the commodore heard of many, many more Englishmen who had been imprisoned and tortured and put in irons, while two, one of them a woman, had even been tortured to death. The commodore became very angry as he listened to Mr. Kincaid's account.

"Why have not these facts been sent to the governor of India?" he asked.

"Every one has been afraid," answered Mr. Kincaid; "for they well knew that had the raywoon heard that a complaint had been made, there would have been ten times as many persons tortured, and ten times as much cruelty done, before ever the Indian government could have sent us help."

Two English merchants were also questioned by Commodore Lambert; and they also told of most frightful cruelties, and proved the truth of what Mr. Kincaid had said.

On Thursday morning four officers were sent on shore with a letter to the governor. The governor was more frightened than ever when he received and read it. He sent at once for Mr. Kincaid. There he sat shaking all over, his face pale and scared, and his voice so trembling he could hardly speak. As he could not read English, the commodore had sent him, with the letter, a translation in Burmese. He showed the letter and the translation to Mr. Kincaid.

"Is this translation right?" he asked.

"Yes," answered Mr. Kincaid, looking at it, "it is quite correct."

"What does it mean?" said the governor. "The letter accuses me of being a bad man, and of committing outrages against the subjects of the queen of England—and yet it does not say what I have done. Tell me what to do."

"I really cannot tell you what to do," replied Mr. Kincaid.

"Don't say so," implored the wretched man. "You have more books and maps than any one else in the town. You know what the English want. Tell me what to do."

"Well," said Mr. Kincaid, "if you do not know what the English want, write a letter to Commodore Lambert, and ask him what he means."

This idea seemed to please the governor. "But," he continued, "tell me, have the English come for peace or for war?"

"They certainly have not come for war, or else instead of two or three ships they would have sent twenty or thirty."

The governor wrote his letter; and as days passed on and no attack was made on the town, though the ships still remained there at anchor, he became less frightened.

Still he collected his troops, and made every preparation he could for fighting. He soon had ten thousand men gathered together; and a very celebrated and desperate robber chief came into the town with all his band to assist the governor. The presence of these soldiers made the town very uncomfortable indeed. They were not orderly troops, as ours are, all under command and obeying their officers. They roamed about much as they liked; and as many of them were accustomed to rob and murder, and were very bold robbers too, you can understand that a great amount of mischief was done by them. They spent their time in plundering the people they ought to have protected, and in ill-using and threatening the Christians. The inhabitants of Rangoon became afraid to sleep in their houses, lest they should be murdered in the night, and for safety hid themselves in all kinds of corners and outhouses. The Burmese officers threatened the Karen Christians especially, and told them that if the English landed and a battle took place, they should be placed in the forefront and shot down first.

Commodore Lambert advised the missionaries, and those foreigners who were able, to leave the town at once, and come on board a merchant vessel which was lying in the river. Mrs. Kincaid and Mrs. Dawson, with the children, did this; but their husbands thought it right to remain on shore as long as they could, and attend to the sick people who came to the dispensary.

One evening, as Mr. Kincaid was walking

in the public street, he was seized by a party of Burmese, and violently dragged into a narrow dark lane, where fifty armed men were lying in wait.

"What do you want with me?" asked Mr. Kincaid; and he reminded them how Commodore Lambert was sure to attack the town if he were ill-treated.

They said he must go with them to the government house. He insisted that they should take him to the customhouse instead; and after a long altercation they did as he bade them. At the customhouse the men were at once ordered to release their prisoner. Mr. Kincaid says that he cannot tell how he managed to get his own way, or how it was that they did not kill him. He must have been very courageous and bold; and there was the Friend above fighting for him, and turning these violent men as He would.

On New Year's day a message arrived from the king. He made great professions of good-will, and said that the governor, who had done so much wrong, should at once be dismissed, and a new viceroy should come to take his place.

In a few days the new governor arrived. He came down the river with twenty or thirty war-boats, all filled with armed men. Three or four hundred of the king's own troops accompanied him from Ava, and many more had joined him on his way down. This did not look much like peace.

When the royal barge, in which was the viceroy, reached the wharf, he was welcomed by the people with great respect. Carpets were spread for him to walk upon, and the carriage in which he was conveyed to his house was drawn by men, while long lines of soldiers in their smartest dresses lined the streets through which he passed. At the government house a party of Brahmins, each man bearing in his hand a horn of plenty, welcomed and blessed him as he entered. Hundreds of the people flocked up during the day with food and fruit for his followers. They had been compelled to supply the servants of the former governor, and supposed they must do the same still. Their offerings, however, were refused; "For," said the viceroy, "the people are poor and in trouble; they cannot afford to give." This was very true, and the new governor won many friends by this kindness and consideration.

The new viceroy had been appointed to the charge not only of Rangoon, but of all the lower provinces of Burmah, from Prome to Martaban. Two or three days passed by, and he took no notice of Commodore Lambert and the English ships, except, indeed, that he forbade any one to go from the shore to the ships.

The commodore sent four officers to visit the governor, carrying with them a letter to his excellency. It was noon when they arrived, and very hot. They were not at once asked into the house, but after several messengers had passed backward and forward, they were informed that the governor was asleep, and could not see them.

"But may we not come in and wait until he wakes?" asked the officers.

"No," was the answer; "you may not come in; if you like to wait, you can walk up and down outside."

This was extremely rude; indeed, it was only another way of saying: "We will have nothing to do with you." You may be very sure the English officers did not walk up and down outside in the scorching sun; they returned at once to the ship, and informed their commander of the insult they had received.

The commodore was very angry; and as it was evident that the professions of good-will had only been made in order to gain time, he determined to wait peaceably no longer, but to show the Burmese that they might expect war if they persisted in ill-treating English subjects.

He sent boats to the shore to bring away all the foreigners who wished for protection, and allowed them only two hours in which to pack up and come away. They came as fast as possible, and brought away whatever they could, but a great many of their things were left behind. However, the loss of their furniture and goods was of little consequence compared with the imprisonment that would be sure to overtake them if they remained longer; and some of them had already sent part of their possessions to the ships.

There was lying in the river a ship of the king's, called "Yâ-theê-nah-yai-moon," which in English means, "The most precious jewel of the ocean." This ship the commodore and his officers agreed to take, in order to show their displeasure. In the night they captured it, without a single shot being fired; and it was towed down the river by the steamer "Hermes."

The next morning the ships prepared to move down the river; but the frigate "Fox" unfortunately ran upon a sand-bank, and was there obliged to wait until the rising tide floated her again. While there, the governor of Dalla, which is on the opposite side of the river to Rangoon, came on board to beg for peace and forgiveness for the viceroy. Commodore Lambert replied that he would think about it, if the viceroy would come to the frigate and apologize for his rudeness to the officers. When the viceroy was asked to do this, however, he refused.

The ships moved down the river with the king's vessel in tow. I suppose the viceroy was afraid his royal master would not be pleased to hear that his "precious jewel" had been taken by the English; for he sent a letter to the commodore to say that the officers were intoxicated when they called upon him, and that was the reason he would not allow them to come in.

This letter was almost immediately followed by a second, with a threat that if "the jewel" were not at once given up, he should order his soldiers to fire on the ships. The commodore replied, he was sorry to hear this. He did not intend making any attack; but if so much as a pistol were fired at the ships he would open the guns and fire back.

A few miles down the river there were some fortifications. Here the governor sent his troops to await the arrival of the ships; and the people of the villages around were ordered to arm and be prepared to seize the "Yä-theê-nah-yai-moon" as it passed.

When the vessels approached the stockades, affairs looked very warlike. Behind the fortifications were men in considerable numbers and guns ready to open fire; while moving about the river were war-boats, in which stood Burmese soldiers singing war-songs and dancing and capering about.

As the "Hermes," with the "precious jewel" in tow, appeared opposite the stockade, it was greeted with a flash and a report from the shore. Immediately the guns of the "Fox" answered, and for two hours a battle was carried on. At one time, through the smoke and confusion, the Burmese boatmen were seen clinging to the sides of their boats, and trying to protect themselves from the ball and shot by keeping all but their heads under water. Soon they left their boats and rushed up the bank to escape. Many were struck down in their flight, and the banks were covered with the dead and dying.

At the end of two hours the firing ceased from the shore; then, too, the ships in the river left off firing; and as the smoke rolled off there were seen the war-boats in which the gay warriors had sung so short a time before deserted and sinking or drifting away. The cannon on shore, too, were deserted; the men who had manned them were either lying by them dead or had run away. There had been terrible slaughter among the poor Burmese. In those two hours not less than three hundred had been killed. But the English were all safe; not one had even a wound; a few musket-balls had indeed hit the "Fox," but she had received no serious injury.

When intelligence of this battle reached the viceroy, he sent messengers with a flag of truce, and a petition from the foreigners imprisoned in Rangoon, in which it was stated that the governor would be willing to make peace on any terms. But it was too late for peace now; an account of the whole affair had been sent to the governor-general of India, and it would remain with him to decide what was to be done.

The missionaries, of course, could not return to Rangoon at present. They went to Maulmain to wait the issue of affairs.

The governor-general, when he received Commodore Lambert's despatches, at once declared war against the Burmese empire; and at the beginning of April an English fleet arrived at the mouths of the Irrawadi. The first place captured was Martaban, which you will find near to Maulmain. Then the fleet sailed up the river and attacked Rangoon. For four days the inhabitants fought with great courage, but it was all in vain; on April 14, 1852, Rangoon fell into the hands of the English, and the rule of the viceroys was at an end for ever.

Mr. Kincaid had come up the river with the fleet, and landed as soon as possible after the city was taken. What a glad welcome he received! How the Christians, Burmese and Karens, flocked around him! From the jungles and hiding-places in which they had concealed themselves they came now, without fear of molestation, to rejoice in their own deliverance and at the sight of their kind teacher. Dr. Dawson and Mr. and Mrs. Vinton soon followed Mr. Kincaid to Rangoon.

In August the governor-general of India, Lord Dalhousie, himself came to Rangoon to arrange the terms of peace with the king. He saw Mr. Kincaid, and inquired about the beginning of the war, and about the dispensary and the Christians—how many Christians there were, and how much good was done by the dispensary. He gave Mr. Kincaid two hundred and fifty rupees for the dispensary, which was again opened, and told him that he hoped affairs might be arranged so as to make the people much happier in future. Before the year ended a proclamation was issued, declaring that Rangoon and the country around belonged no more to the king of Ava; but that the whole of Pegu, from Maulmain to Arracan, from the seacoast inland to Prome, should be in future part of the empire of British India.

CHAPTER XXX.

THE GOSPEL SPREADING IN RANGOON AND THE COUNTRY AROUND.

IT was in the year 1852 that Pegu was taken from the king of Burmah and made part of the dominions of the queen of England. Most of the people were very glad on account of the change of government, for they were quite tired of the oppressions practised by their native rulers, and hoped that now brighter days would dawn. To the Karens especially it was a very happy change. One old man exclaimed: "Oh, how I wish I could see the queen of England! how I would worship her!"

As soon as Pegu was freed from its tyrant rulers, the American missionaries in Burmah met together at Maulmain to decide who should go to Rangoon and the other towns now open to them. It was arranged that missionaries should be stationed at Rangoon, Bassein, Tounghoo, Shwaygheen, Henthada, and Prome, at all which places many of those who had been idolaters were eagerly longing for teachers.

After the meeting at Maulmain, the missionaries at Rangoon were joined by Mr. and Mrs. Ingalls, who had for some years been stationed at Akyab. Very interesting accounts Mrs. Ingalls has sent home from Rangoon, but I must only give you the story of one man; it is in Mrs. Ingall's own words:

"It was noonday. The sun was pouring down its scorching rays, making it one of the hot days of Burmah. The poor Burman dog had dug his bed under the shadow of a shrub or beneath the ladder steps. The house-cat had left her wonted sunny bed, and sought a resting place close by the water-jar; and most of the natives had sought a shelter from the rays of the scorching sun. Even the parrot-bird drooped its green wings, and clung to the very bottom of his cage for a shadow.

"At this hour a Burman of about thirty-five years of age might have been seen slowly plodding his way to the city. For a turban he wore some four yards of the finest book-muslin. His jacket was of jaconet; and a piece of fine blue plaided silk was wound round his body and limbs, and was fastened in front by a loose knot, allowing the ends to hang down in a graceful fold. His feet were encased in green sandals, and he carried over his head a leaf-umbrella. His outer appearance was that of a respectable Burman. He walked slowly along, seemingly unconscious of the excessive heat, though he was evidently suffering from it. He scarcely raised his eyes from beneath his knitted brow, and only paused a moment at the door of a hovel to relight his cigar ere he entered the town.

"He passed on; but suddenly his footsteps were arrested by the hand of a familiar friend beckoning him to enter the zayat in which he was sitting. He hesitated a moment, and turning round, gazed at the poor bamboo hovels which he had just passed; and then, turning again, he ran his eye along the group of zayats and monasteries, and then lifting his eye to their graduated roofs, with their curious carvings and glittering spires, gazed on the golden pagoda in the centre and the tall flagstaffs interspersed here and there, from which float the long gauze streamers which point the people to the holy place. The Burman seemed lost in thought as he compared the wretched bamboo hovels and the splendor of the scene before him, and the call of his friend was unheeded.

"'Why do you not come and visit us? Are you becoming Jesus Christ's man?'

"The last words struck upon his ear, and he turned his feet to the zayat, assuring his friend he was not Jesus Christ's man. The yellow-robed priests in the zayat relighted their cigars, which had wasted from their long slumbers, adjusted their pillows, and with their strings of black beads, which answer the purpose of rosaries, placed themselves in the attitude of listeners.

"The old Burman pushed the cup of water to the traveller, Moung Shway Pau, and then began his inquiries of 'Where have you been? Do you think the white foreigners will drive us from our home? Why have you not attended our feasts and made offerings to our gods of late?'

"'The bells are falling from the pagoda,'

THE PRIEST'S APPEAL.

answered Moung Shway Pau, dissembling as he spoke, 'and it needs regilding. The people are getting slack, I fear—becoming heretics; for I hear the American teachers are daily receiving the calls of many of our people, and I often see them with those little books. One of the heretics passed here a few days since with a large bundle of tracts, and pressed me to take one; but I quickly told him I would not soil my hands with one of them. He attempted to leave one; but I told him I would make kites for the children of it; so he left, saying his God could open my heart without books.'

"Seven or eight of the priests had jealously watched the countenance of Moung Shway Pau, and conjectured that he knew more of those books than he admitted; so they drew near, and in their sacred language expatiated long on the beauties of their religion. They pressed him to seek for merit, and told him if he would only replace one of those soiled book-muslin streamers which floated on the breeze he would get great merit. As many times as it floated on the breeze, so many times he would be king of the earth.

"He could not conceal his contempt for this folly, and told them: 'Yes, it was only the natural course of things; if he hung his head-dress on the staff it would float, if there was any breeze.' Then adjusting his silken garment, and carefully concealing a small book which he had in the fold, he left; and a half hour's walk brought him to his abode.

"His sister unrolled a mat for him, and his nephew, a boy six years old, with a good share of the milk of human kindness beaming from his eye, stumbled over the mat, spilling the cup of water which he was wishing to give his uncle.

"A smile lit up the face of Moung Shway Pau as he picked up the little boy; but his brow instantly became knitted, and throwing himself upon his mat, he pressed his aching head, and sighed deeply. His sister, Mah Doke, brought in her vegetables, and began dressing them for the evening meal. As she glanced at her brother, she saw from the quick heaving of his bosom that he was troubled, and throwing down her knife, she was soon at his side, asking him if he were ill.

"He replied 'No' and 'Yes' in the same breath; and then said he did not believe their god could save them from hell. Their religion was all give, give; and he saw they could only receive poverty in return for all their gifts, and after death go down to hell. 'I wish to worship the God who can save me from hell.'

"'What!' exclaimed the sister, her eye flashing with shame and anger, 'will you leave the religion of your forefathers for that of the foreigners? Will you bring shame and disgrace upon your sister?' And she returned to her cooking.

"Moung Shway Pau now drew from the folds of his dress a small book, which he carefully opened, and began perusing with eagerness. It was the gospel of Luke; and he read: 'Whosoever shall be ashamed of me and of my words, of him shall the Son of man be ashamed, when he shall come in his own glory, and in his Father's, and of the holy angels.'

"The tears rushed to his eyes, and he smote his breast vehemently, saying: 'I denied thee—was ashamed of thee at the kyoung—and I must go down to hell. I believe, O God, thou art the only true God; yet I denied thee there.'

"Moung Shway Pau sought his mat; but it was not to sleep—his mind was too busy with the past and present. His sins rose up before him as a thick cloud, and he groaned and wept in the bitterness of his soul, crying: 'God be merciful to me a sinner!' He spent the night in deep repentance before God, and only closed his eyes just as the sun began to shed its first feeble rays of light.

"He was, however, soon aroused from his slumbers by the shouts of the people and the tramp of multitudes. It was the waning of the moon, the day of worship for the followers of Gaudama. Business had been suspended, and young and old were busy in paying homage at the temples of Gaudama, and presenting offerings of rice and fruit and flowers. The people were dressed in their best attire, loaded with yellow cotton cloth and silk. Every now and then were borne upon the shoulders of men small trees with hundreds of branches, from which hung handkerchiefs, pillows, mats, umbrellas, cups, flowers, fruits, and candles—offerings for the priests—the whole producing a bright and gorgeous scene.

"These days had been the delight of Moung Shway Pau, and he had been wont to exult with pride over all this display, when he compared it with the humble worship of the foreigners and the heretics; but now his heart sickened at the sight. He had firmly resolved to become a Christian; and as the sun arose, he hastened to the foreign teachers to receive instruction, and to tell them of his wish to worship the eternal God. The teacher's heart beat with joy as he heard the glad news. The native teachers were called together, and they all sought the mercy-seat. God was with them, and Moung Shway Pau became a rejoicing convert."

Mr. Ingalls did not remain many years in Rangoon; his heavenly Father called him away from his work. Mrs. Ingalls, when she lost her husband, thought of returning to America with her little girl; but the people so begged her to remain with them that she consented. One said: "If you will stay, I will do any thing for you." Another offered the posts for a house, and another boards for the floor. One poor man, who could offer neither posts nor boards, held up his two brown hands and said: "Here, mamma, is my gift; they are strong, and can help make the house, if you will only stay." And she stayed with these poor, loving, Christian people, in a part of Rangoon called Kemmendine, and there opened a girls' school, to which they gladly sent their daughters.

Mr. and Mrs. Vinton had been at Tavoy before going to Rangoon. At Rangoon they remained for six years. During that time they labored with great success. They constantly made tours into the villages around; and in many of the hamlets little knots of Christians were formed into churches, while schools were opened for the children. By the end of the six years forty-two chapels and thirty schools were opened; and in the chapels eight or nine thousand persons met every Sabbath to worship God, while a hundred native Christians had been trained as teachers and pastors.

This was the account ten years ago, when Mr. Vinton was called to his rest in heaven. Now, to-day, those chapels and schools are full, and are resounding with the praises of God. More chapels and schools, too, have been built; and this not only in Rangoon, but in other parts of Burmah also.

Mr. Kincaid did not remain at Rangoon; he went to Prome. In the villages around Prome many Karens have now become Christians; and where quarrelling and wickedness prevailed may now be heard the sweet singing of the praises of Jesus, in which men and women and little children unite.

In 1858 Mr. Kincaid tells us he had the pleasure of baptizing a young Burman who had been at the head of one of the kyoungs. He was a very clever young man, and understood Buddhism better than most Buddhists. One day a native Christian entered the kyoung, and spoke to this priest about God's Son who had come from heaven. But instead of listening, he ordered the man to be turned out of the house. Not long after, the Christian ventured again to the kyoung, and the priest was so surprised by his perseverance and kindness that this time he listened. He listened, and wished to hear more. He took some parts of the New Testament which the good Christian had given him, and sat down to read them. He read them again and again.

He told the other priests in the kyoung of these new truths that he was learning; for they had taken such possession of his heart that he felt compelled to speak of them. In a few months he flung away his yellow robes, came out of the kyoung, and declared himself a disciple of Jesus.

The kyoung had been built and was supported by the people of four villages. How astonished were these villagers to hear their priest preach to them Jesus! They had called this man their lord and master, and had constantly brought him offerings of their possessions; but now he read in God's holy word: "One is your Master, even Christ; and all ye are brethren;" and he desired that the people around should serve only the Saviour who had died for him and for them.

CHAPTER XXXI.

DR. AND MRS. MASON REMOVE TO TOUNGHOO—SKETCH OF SAU QUALA.

DR. MASON had been laboring at Tavoy ever since the time of Mr. Boardman's death in 1831, and one of his first works had been, the translation of the Bible into the Karen language. His first wife had died, and he had married the widow of Mr. Bullard, who had been stationed at Dong-yahn.

Now, in 1853, Dr. and Mrs. Mason left Tavoy in the care of other missionaries, and removed to Tounghoo. Tounghoo is an old city, situated on the river Sittang, but until it was annexed to the English provinces, at the close of the war of which you have heard, no missionary had been there to reside. There were in the Tounghoo district as many as thirty thousand Karens, and in the country adjoining not less than two hundred thousand more.

None of these Karens had heard of the true God, or could read his word; but as soon as the missionaries arrived, the good news of the white foreigners with God's book spread among them and caused great joy.

"One day," Mrs. Mason says, "there came in a tall light-brown chieftain, with large, melancholy eyes, and an uncommonly pleasing countenance, habited in a striped cotton tunic, girded around him like a Highland kilt. His long, black, shaggy hair was half-confined by a narrow red turban, and a curious-shaped basket was hung over his back. He carried a long bamboo spear, which served both for a weapon and a staff. Eight or ten swarthy mountaineers, attired like himself, accompanied him.

"'Has God's Son come down from heaven, lady? A man told us so in the mountains, and we have come to see him.'

"'Yes, brother; but—'

"'Where is he?' interrupting with eager eyes. 'Is he here? In Rangoon? In Bengala? Tell us quick, lady, for we have come to see him!'

"'He has come—sit down, brother—he has come, but he is not here. He is gone back to heaven; but—'

"Instantly the tall chieftain turned and strode away with all his followers.

"'Stop! stop, brother! he has left a letter for you!' I called after him.

"No answer. On he goes, and disappears."

In about a week this chieftain returned, and heard more of God's Son; but Dr. Mason could not remain to tell the thousands of Karens the good news they were longing for.

He was ill when he went to Tounghoo, and though he recovered for a time, the following year he became so much worse that he was compelled to leave his mission work and take a long voyage for the benefit of his health. He first went to London with his wife, and they afterwards visited America together.

It was a trouble to Dr. and Mrs. Mason to be obliged to leave Tounghoo so soon after entering upon their work there. But were the thousands of Karens to be left without a teacher? No; in Tavoy was another man, a

Karen, who, before Dr. Mason left for England, came gladly to tell his Tounghoo brothers the joyful tidings he had learned.

This man's name was Sau Quala. His parents had lived near Tavoy; but though their hut was built in a beautiful spot of God's fair earth, and it might have been a happy home, their Burmese neighbors had sorely oppressed and persecuted them.

About the time that their little son was born they heard that the white foreigners had come over the water with God's book, and they called their baby Quala, or hope, because they hoped that happiness would come to them in his day.

Quala grew up in his father's hut by the beautiful waterfall; and it was when he was about fifteen years old that Tavoy was taken by the English. That was in the first Burmese war, when Dr. Judson was made a prisoner.

One day Quala, with his father and mother, went into the town. For some reason, they were taken to the government house; and this alarmed them dreadfully. But the English governor, instead of ill-treating them, spoke kindly, and gave them presents of money and a new turban apiece. Kind words and presents were not often given to the Karens; was the happiness for which they had hoped really coming?

A year or two after a stranger visited Quala's home. He came with tidings of a God of love, who would save from sin and death. The tidings sank down into young Quala's heart, and he said: "Is not this the very thing we have been waiting for?"

That stranger was Kothahbyn. He had lately come to Tavoy with Mr. Boardman; and one of the very first houses he entered was the house of Quala's father.

But though the son believed, the father did not, and he so violently opposed the young man that Quala was afraid to go into Tavoy and hear Mr. Boardman preach. Indeed, so unkind was his father to him, that at last poor Quala was tempted to give up the new religion altogether, and said to himself: "I will never go to the teacher as long as I live, and I will pray no more. When the righteous One appears, my father will suffer himself, and I will say: 'I did not dare to become a Christian on account of my father." And when telling about this sad time, Sau Quala says: "I felt very unhappy. I wept all day, and thought I would starve myself to death."

But better thoughts came, and after a time Sau Quala left his father's house and went to live with his brother on the other side of the mountain.

After the rebellion in Tavoy, when Mr. Boardman returned so ill and weak, Sau Quala was one of those Karens who came into the town to see him, and ask to be baptized. Then he remained near the dying missionary; he helped to carry him during that last journey into the jungle; he was one of those who lifted him so tenderly into the boat, and at last conveyed him to the grave.

Sau Quala returned no more to his old forest life. He stayed with Dr. Mason, both in order to learn from him and to assist him in his work. For a short time he went to one of the schools near Maulmain; but this was only for three months. He came back to Tavoy, and for many years was a great help to Dr. Mason, not only in preaching the gospel among the Karens, but also in finding out the stories and traditions they believed, and writing them down. In this way he made books for his countrymen.

At the end of fifteen years passed in this manner, Sau Quala was made a pastor, and took charge of a Karen congregation at a place called Pyeekhya.

Ten years before this he and Dr. Mason had, on one occasion, been there together, and from a hill-top had looked down on the Karen hamlets lying below them in the valley.

"When," said Dr. Mason, "shall these valleys resound with the songs of the redeemed?"

"Hereafter, teacher, hereafter!" Sau Quala had answered.

And now at the end of ten years they stood in the same spot, and saw below them little chapels and school-houses, and knew that hundreds of Christians were dwelling there.

"God will do greater things than these," said Quala, "until all Burmah worships the eternal God."

But in a few years more Dr. Mason removed from Tavoy and went to Tounghoo, and Sau Quala also left the peaceful valley of Pyeekhya. Dr. and Mrs. Mason were obliged to leave the work at Tounghoo for a time in Sau Quala's hands; and God blessed this good and earnest man wonderfully, and showed him greater things in Tounghoo than had been seen even in Tavoy.

"Because God has showed me my work," says Sau Quala, "I rest not. I go up the mountains and down the valleys, hither and thither. One day in one place, one night in a place, continually. Still I know that I do the work of God imperfectly, and my heart is exceeding sad. Some come to me from a distance, and reprove me, saying: 'Teacher, thou sayest thou hast come to exhort men, and thou hast not been to our stream—to our land. Dost thou not love us?"

Quala did love the Karens. He loved them more than money or honor; for Major Phayre, who had been appointed commissioner of Pegu, asked him to become overseer of the Karens at Tounghoo, and promised him money if he would undertake the office; but he refused. Sau Quala gave the following account of his interview with Major Phayre:

"The commissioner arrived at Tounghoo

on the 9th of March, and I went immediately to visit him. He shook hands with me, and asked me concerning the different tribes of Karens; and in respect to their listening and becoming Christians, and concerning all the unordained assistants; and finally he said:

"'Teacher, I have spoken to the government about you, that you should become the head and overseer among the wild Karens, for which you shall receive thirty rupees a month.'

"I replied: 'Sir, I cannot do it. I will not have the money. I will not mix up God's work with government work. There are others to do this thing. Employ them. As for me, I will continue in the work in which I have engaged.'

"The commissioner asked: 'Where do you obtain money to live on? Why do you not like money? We will give money, and you may continue your work as a teacher as heretofore. Will it not make it easier for you?'

"I answered: 'No, sir. When I eat with the children of poverty, my heart sleeps (that is, I am content). I did not leave my dear wife and come up hither in search of silver, or agreeable food. I came to this land that its poor benighted inhabitants might be saved. Be patient with me, sir. Were I to take your money, the wild Karens would turn against me.'

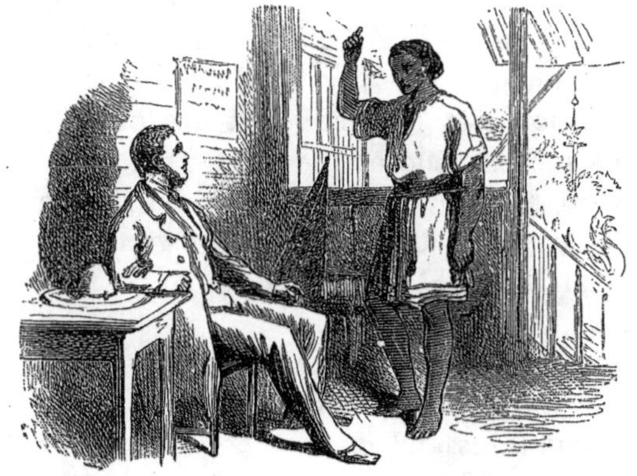

"He said to me again: 'Well, teacher. Think of the matter a day or two.'

"So I left him, and I went to the Christian chief Kwailai, and the Shan who had been baptized, and I persuaded them to take the office.

"The next day I visited the commissioner

again, and presented these two men, as willing to receive the appointment. He agreed to give them the office; so I am free with clean hands."

For two years and a half Sau Quala pursued his missionary work at Tounghoo, and at the end of that time Dr. and Mrs. Mason returned from America with recruited health. What a change those years had wrought! The missionaries had received accounts of Quala's success, and of the rapid progress of the work they had commenced; but, when they arrived at Tounghoo, they were surprised and bewildered at the change they beheld.

A missionary writing about this time says: "Three years and a half ago I gazed over these mountains and plains where the fallen angels have held supreme power ever since the days of Noah, wondering if there were any of the chosen among them. Now our missionary boatman Shapan stands beside me, pointing to the north, south, east, and west, and says:

"'Teacheress, among these hills and valleys there are ninety-six churches, ninety-six chapels, ninety-six Christian schools, and two thousand six hundred baptized converts.'

"The tidings were perfectly bewildering—men who, three years before, had never heard of Jesus!

"Three years ago I looked upon troop after troop of wild mountaineers, with their short striped gowns and unwashed faces, wondering if they could be civilized. Now I look upon a hundred young men and lads, all neatly dressed, in clean new gowns, and blue trousers, with their hair nicely braided under tasteful turbans.

"Three years ago I sent to them the first book they ever saw in their own tongue. Yesterday, I sat in the midst of twenty young preachers, fine intelligent youths, all following the speaker with open Bibles, turning from page to page, from paragraph to paragraph with perfect ease and the deepest interest. I could but exclaim: 'What hath God wrought!'

"Near Tounghoo is a very warlike tribe of Karens called Bghais, and when Dr. Mason first settled there, it was a question who would venture among them as a teacher of

Christianity. Shapan was asked who should go.

"'I don't know,' he replied, and sat for some minutes in deep thought: then looking up very sadly and timidly, he said:

"'I wish I knew enough to go to the Bghais.'

"'Perhaps you do; or if not, God can make you know enough,' Dr. Mason answered."

It was decided that Shapan knew enough, if he were willing to go. Mrs. Mason reminded him that he would be obliged to leave his child and his home, and that besides this he would have very little money. He received fifteen rupees a month as Dr. Mason's boatman; as a Christian teacher to the Bghais he would only have four.

"Would you go for that?" Mrs. Mason asked.

Shapan did not answer; he took up his Testament and went out. After a time he returned with a radiant face.

"Well, Shapan," said Dr. Mason; "what is your decision? Can you go to the Bghais for four rupees a month?"

"No, teacher," answered Shapan solemnly; "I could not go for four rupees a month. But I can do it for Christ."

And for Christ's sake Shapan did go.

But I must not continue these stories. A most interesting account of the Tounghoo mission and schools you may read in a book entitled "Civilizing Mountain Men."

These missions in Burmah, of which you have been reading, have been supported by the Christians in America with both money and prayers: and the Karens, who by thousands have been converted to God, have not been ungrateful, nor have they forgotten to what land they were indebted. Now they do much to support their teachers themselves, and for many of them no help is asked from America. I will conclude with a letter that Sau Quala wrote to the American Christians after the return of Dr. and Mrs. Mason to Tounghoo:

"Dear friends, I am Quala, a wild man, a son of the forest, an uncultivated one, who neither knows nor understands anything. I a dark-minded, unworthy one, send you salutation. I am not your equal, yet through the grace of God I call you brethren.

"Dear friends, you truly abound in ability, in patient endurance, in love, in mercy, and goodness. Behold, my dear friends, had you not sent the teachers and teacheresses to us wild men, the sons of the East, living in darkness, we should have gone on to destruction both in this world and the world to come for ever.

"Dear friends, the grace that the white foreigners, the sons of America, have displayed is so much, so great, that it cannot be expressed by words. It is exceedingly great, for you have saved us from death. Formerly we knew not God, we had no books, and being destitute of instruction, we knew nothing.

"When you sent the teachers and teacheresses among us, and they told us that God loved the world so much that he gave us his Son Jesus Christ, who came and purchased us by his blood, we became Christians, and became able to discern between right and wrong; and when the teachers made us books our knowledge increased greatly. Still, the signification, the reason of things, we understood very imperfectly, and we should never have known had not the teachers and teacheresses taught us, and explained them to us; because, my dear friends, we are habituated to darkness, and things of light we understand with great difficulty. Still some make their ears crooked, will not give attention, and do not believe, but, on the contrary, revile. Pray to God for them, that they may repent, believe, obtain new hearts, and all become disciples, like ourselves.

"God has now displayed his power in Tounghoo, and many sons of the forest, living in darkness, have believed, and your kindness is great in sending two teachers to help them. As to myself, being of a race of uncultivated men, I am of no value.

"When I was fifteen years of age, English white rulers, the sons of the West, reached this country of Burmah, and my father and mother said: 'Now happiness has reached the land! They have come by water. Children, you have fallen on the time when they arrived.' After a short interval, the American teacher Boardman came, when many believed, and I was baptized. I studied a very long time in the hands of teacher Mason, and I came to know and understand the truth as one in a dream. Still I became a teacher to go about preaching and administering baptism.

"This was through your kindness, for when I was studying with teacher Mason, you sent the money which you gave to teacher Mason. My relatives were unable to support me, and, had it not been for your money, I could not have studied, nor by any means have acquired the knowledge I have.

"When I think of your kindness I feel as if I could not extol it sufficiently. Though I die I will praise your goodness to my children and grandchildren, and the generation following. I am now growing old, my hair is gray, my sight dim, and through sickness my strength has failed, so that I have not the vigor I had when I studied with teacher Mason; but my strength in God has not decreased in the least. Pray for me.

"The favor you have shown me, my dear friends, is exceedingly great. When teacher Mason and the teacheress returned to America, I told them the things I would like to have, and they procured the whole of them. They obtained for me black alpaca two suits, a white blanket, with many other articles of clothing, and a spy-glass of the very best kind, besides a large quantity of medicine. I also received, through your kindness, a cloak from teacher Cross.

"But, brethren, we have received not worldly things of you merely, we have received spiritual things also, and can never forget you. Though I cannot speak with you personally, yet my love and remembrance of you is uninterrupted, and I hope to be able to converse with you in the kingdom of God, and associate with you eternally. My dear friends, the greatest favors you have shown us are sending us teachers and teacheresses, who came and taught us the word of God, made books for us, taught us figures, and instructed us in the things of light.

"Through the power of God, may your towns and cities, your lands and waters, your kingdom and domain, your houses and dwellings, your plans and devices, your works and deeds be established, increased, and perfected in goodness, happiness, and light, generation on generation for ever.

"TEACHER QUALA,

"A SON OF THE FOREST,

"July 26th, 1857."

The Karens are still pressing into the kingdom of God. But we—you and I—are we pressing in also? We, who have been taught to pray: "Thy kingdom come. Thy will be done on earth as it is in heaven;" are we among the children of the kingdom? Or, while we pray this prayer, and drop our pence into the missionary box, are we still outside? It is a very, very serious question, and we must, each one of us, answer it for ourselves.

Listen to what Jesus says: "Strive to enter in at the strait gate: for many, I say unto you, will seek to enter in, and shall not be able. When once the master of the house is risen up, and hath shut to the door, and ye begin to stand without, and to knock at the door, saying: Lord, Lord, open unto us. And he shall answer and say unto you: I know you not whence ye are. Then shall ye begin to say: We have eaten and drunk in thy presence, and thou hast taught in our streets. But he shall say: I tell you, I know you not whence ye are; depart from me, all ye workers of iniquity. There shall be weeping and gnashing of teeth, when ye shall see

Abraham, and Isaac, and Jacob, and all the prophets in the kingdom of God, and you yourselves thrust out. And they shall come from the East, and from the West, and from the North, and from the South, and shall sit down in the kingdom of God. And behold, there are last which shall be first, and there are first which shall be last."

Do you wish to be in God's kingdom and not thrust out? Jesus says: "Him that cometh unto me, I will in no wise cast out."

It is more than eighteen hundred years since, in the clear, midnight sky, angels sang: "Fear not; for behold, I bring you good tidings of great joy, which shall be to all people. For unto you is born this day, in the city of David, a Saviour, which is Christ the Lord. Glory to God in the highest, on earth peace, good will toward men."

And now, after eighteen hundred years, the echo of the angels' song, which has never quite slumbered, is waking up. From north to south, from east to west, may be caught the sounds of that new and heavenly song, the echo, and explanation, and completion of what the angels sang: "Thou art worthy, for thou wast slain, and hast redeemed us to God by thy blood out of every kindred, and tongue, and people, and nation; and hast made us unto our God kings and priests, and we shall reign on the earth."

Let us join in that glad song with all our hearts.

www.ingramcontent.com/pod-product-compliance
Lightning Source LLC
LaVergne TN
LVHW020216110826
845151LV00003B/737
9781425533670